Wonder Kids

The Remarkable Lives of Nine Child Prodigies

by Charis Cotter

annick press
toronto + new york + vancouver

©2008 Charis Cotter (text)
Edited by Barbara Pulling
Design: Sheryl Shapiro

We acknowledge the support of the Canada Council for the Arts, the Government of Canada through the Book Publishing Industry Development Program (BPIDP) for our publishing activities, and the Ontario Arts Council.

 ONTARIO ARTS COUNCIL
CONSEIL DES ARTS DE L'ONTARIO

Cataloging in Publication

Cotter, Charis
    Wonder kids : the remarkable lives of nine child prodigies / Charis Cotter.

Includes bibliographical references and index.
ISBN 978-1-55451-133-4 (pbk.)
ISBN 978-1-55451-134-1 (bound)

    1. Gifted children—Biography—Juvenile literature. I. Title.

CT107.C72 2008   j920.0087'9   C2007-905115-4

Distributed in Canada by:

Firefly Books Ltd.
66 Leek Crescent
Richmond Hill, ON
L4B 1H1

Published in the U.S.A. by:

Annick Press (U.S.) Ltd.
Distributed in the U.S.A. by:
Firefly Books (U.S.) Inc.
P.O. Box 1338
Ellicott Station
Buffalo, NY 14205

Printed in China.

Visit us at: www.annickpress.com

For Beni, always a wonder kid
—C.C.

ACKNOWLEDGMENTS

Beni Malone's enthusiasm for Buster Keaton sparked the idea for *Wonder Kids*, and it grew into a book with the expert help of all my friends at Annick. I am very grateful to the Ontario Arts Council for the grants that made it possible for me to write this book. Françoise Vulpe used her detective skills to help with some of the more obscure research, and she also gave me the idea to write about Phillis Wheatley. Thanks to Terry Tao for introducing me to his father, and many heartfelt thanks to Billy Tao, who graciously provided me with a wealth of material about Terry's childhood and answered my many questions.

I pinched the title for Terry's chapter from his website and several newspaper articles that dubbed him "The Mozart of Math." Barbara Pulling should get a medal for her superb editing: like a compass she kept me on track. Julien Procuta gave me some thoughtful feedback. My daughter Zoe listened to all my dilemmas and gave me suggestions and steady encouragement while my parents cheered me on with their usual enthusiasm and brought me cheese. And finally, thanks to all the wonder kids themselves, who continue to inspire me with their exuberance, their dedication, and their passion.

—Charis Cotter

IMAGE CREDITS

CONTENTS

INTRODUCING THE WONDER KIDS

What if you were so good at something that people called you a child prodigy? What would your life be like? Imagine a theater crowded with grown-ups listening to you play the piano, or watching you bounce off walls onstage as a pint-sized acrobat. How would it feel to have a hit record, or your own art exhibition at a big museum? What if you were so good at card tricks that you could hoodwink famous magicians? Or so clever at math that you could start university at age nine?

In this book you will meet nine kids whose amazing abilities transformed the world around them. Clara Schumann played the piano so brilliantly at 11 that sophisticated audiences in Paris flocked to see her. When Fanny Mendelssohn was 13, she memorized two hours of Bach's piano music and then performed it superbly as a birthday present for her father. Phillis Wheatley, a black slave, published her first poem when she was 14. Maria Agnesi spoke seven languages by the time she was 13. Buster Keaton was hurtling through the air on the vaudeville stage when he was three, and Dai Vernon fooled a world-renowned magician with a card trick at age seven. Stevie Wonder drove fans wild with his fantastic harmonica solos when he was 12, and Wang Yani painted such life-like and playful monkeys that her work was being shown all over the world by the time she was 10. Terry Tao was six when he wrote his first computer program. These children all had something exceptional inside them that shone so brightly the grown-up world stopped to take notice.

Most kids know how it feels to be good at something, whether it's hockey, playing the drums, spelling, or throwing a baseball. And it's easy to become fascinated by a subject and want to learn everything about it—perhaps dinosaurs, or ancient Egypt, or medieval knights, or outer space. But think about combining the ability to do

something really well with a passionate desire to spend all your time doing it. These wonder kids had brains and talent to burn, and many of them had parents or other sympathetic adults who made it possible for them to live up to their potential.

Scientific studies have shown that the brains of child prodigies are different from ordinary brains. For a long time, people believed that children this unusual had been given special gifts from God. But although it might seem like predestination or magic, child prodigies have to make sacrifices to realize their dreams. The children in this book all worked harder than normal kids do, and they missed out on some of the fun of childhood. It takes a tough, dedicated kid to practice or study for hours each day, go on long tours away from home, and sometimes deal with parents' unreasonable demands for perfection. The payoff was the joy and satisfaction these gifted children found in working at what they loved best.

All these kids had to learn very quickly how to live in an adult world. Grown-ups were fascinated by the mystery of their exceptional abilities and lavished praise on them. Sometimes they were treated as super-humans, almost like freaks. But they were still children, faced with all the usual challenges of growing up. They had messy rooms, talked back to their parents, fought with their brothers and sisters, and struggled to find out how they fit into the world.

Wonder Kids explores the lives of nine young people: how their talent was discovered, how it was developed, and how they used their gifts as they grew up. The settings for these stories range from Boston in the 1760s to China in the 1970s, from the Enlightenment in Italy to the birth of Motown in Detroit, from Germany in the 19th century to Australia in the 20th. But no matter where or when they lived, all these children had something in common: they were wonder kids who made a lasting impact on the world.

A VOICE FROM CAPTIVITY

PHILLIS WHEATLEY NEGRO SERVANT to Mr JOHN WHEATLEY, of BOSTON.

Published according to Act of Parliament, Sept. 1, 1773 by Arch.d Bell,

Bookseller N° 8 near the Saracens Head Aldgate.

Phillis Wheatley

1753–1784

P hillis couldn't breathe. The darkness pressed against her chest as she gasped painfully for air. The ship rolled back and forth in the endless swell of the sea. Someone was moaning. She tried another breath, and drew in the rancid smell of people confined in too small a space without toilets or water for washing. "I must keep breathing," she told herself fiercely. "One breath after another until this is over." But the heavy blackness bore down upon her as the ship rocked from side to side, and her stomach heaved ...

Phillis sat up in bed, her heart racing. The room was dark. She took a long, shuddering breath and the pressure in her chest lifted a bit. Then she groped on the table beside her for matches and lit the candle.

A warm yellow light formed a circle around the candle flame, like a little sun. Phillis looked around her room. It was all familiar and safe. Her apron hung over the back of the chair, and on the desk by the window sat a neat pile of paper, her quill pen, and a bottle of ink.

Phillis's asthma was bad tonight. And the dream was back. She had been free of it for months, and she had hoped it was gone for good. When the Wheatleys first brought her to this big house, the dream had come every single night. No matter how kind the family were to her during the day, at night she returned in her sleep to that stinking ship. After many weeks, as Phillis adjusted to her new life, the nightmare had gradually faded.

But tonight she had been sharply reminded of those long weeks crossing the Atlantic—the storms that came from nowhere, the howling winds whipping the ocean to a frenzy. She remembered how fear had gripped her heart in the midst of those storms, convincing her that she was about to die.

Phillis had been thrown back to that time, now seven years past, by the harrowing tale told by two visitors at supper. Mr. Hussey and Mr. Coffin had survived a gale that nearly destroyed their ship, and Phillis took in every word as she served them boiled potatoes and roast chicken. In fact, she was so caught up in their story that she forgot to serve the peas until Mrs. Wheatley gently reminded her.

And now she couldn't get the pictures out of her mind. She saw the men thrown from one side of the ship to the other, clutching at ropes, shouting for help. She saw the waves rear up like huge dark monsters, hungry to swallow the little ship. Words started tumbling through her mind, words to describe the terror, the darkness, the raging wind. The room was filled with the creak of straining timber, the crack of sails snapping, the crash of thunder, and a sudden flash of lightning that split the mast in two. "God save us!" cried the men.

"Enough!" said Phillis, throwing back the cozy quilt and sitting up. The floor was cold on her bare feet as she rushed over to her desk and dipped her pen in the ink. She began to write.

> Did Fear and Danger so perplex your Mind
> As made you fearful of the Whistling Wind?

The words that had been whirling in her head took form on the paper, painting a picture of the storm and the frightened sailors. Sometimes she paused and closed her eyes, searching for a rhyme or a better word. She knew if she waited, the words would come. She loved the way they formed a pattern on the page, line after line, bringing order to the chaos inside her.

Time slipped away. The house was very quiet. A clock downstairs chimed off the hours, and occasionally there was noise from the street outside. With her head bent over the page, her hair illuminated by the soft candlelight, Phillis was lost in the creation of her poem.

She didn't realize it, but Phillis Wheatley was making history. The poem would later appear in a local paper, the first of her many poems to be published. Phillis was the first African-American poet, at the age of 14. She was also a slave.

KIDNAPPED

The little girl later known as Phillis Wheatley began her life with an African name and family. She lived somewhere in west Africa, in the region of Gambia or Senegal, a fertile countryside with many small villages and abundant fish and food. When she was about seven, she was kidnapped by slave traders and shipped across the Atlantic Ocean to Boston. She never saw her parents again. The horrors she survived were so shocking that she forgot everything about her early life, except for one shining image: her mother welcoming the rising sun by lifting a gourd full of water to the sky and then pouring the water out onto the ground.

We will never know exactly how Phillis came to be kidnapped. Different forms of slavery had been practiced in parts of Africa for hundreds of years. By the time Phillis was born, in about 1753, it had grown into a huge, profitable industry, fueled by the demand for slaves in the West Indies and the Americas. Phillis may have strayed away from her village and been snatched by a gang of slave traders. Or they might have invaded her village and taken the inhabitants by force, killing those who resisted. The prisoners were marched to the coast, where they were sold to a slave ship.

Big men shoved Phillis into the hold of the ship along with other women and children. A few African men were there too, chained together. The hold was dark and smelly, with the ship forever rocking in the swells of the sea. Many people got seasick. Others cried inconsolably. They were being torn away from their homes and families, and the word quickly spread that they were going to a faraway country where they would be slaves all their lives. In despair, some people refused to eat, and some watched for a chance to throw themselves overboard to drown. But little Phillis clung to life, even though she was sick with asthma, cold, and hungry for most of the trip, with only a little rice to eat and water to drink. Somehow she survived this terrible ordeal with her strength of character and keen intelligence intact.

The Slave Trade

In the 18th century, the slave trade was a booming business; millions of captives were shipped across the Atlantic Ocean. They came from several different African countries. Some were prisoners of war, but most were abducted.

Today it is hard to understand how people could treat their fellow human beings so badly. We recognize that everyone has the right to be free. But in the 18th century, many white people told themselves that black people lacked intelligence as well as feelings, and that they were born to be slaves. Some even claimed they were doing black people a favor by providing them with food and shelter.

However, not everyone thought this way. An anti-slavery movement had begun in Europe and was spreading to North America. In 1772 all slaves in England were freed. But slavery would not be completely abolished in the British Empire and its colonies until 1833, and it was still legal in some American states until 1865.

The captain was dissatisfied with his cargo. He wanted more men, because they fetched higher prices than women or children, but he had been sailing down the coast for weeks with little success. He finally gave up and headed home for Boston, to make the most of what he had: about 80 Africans. It was lucky for Phillis that the captain could not fill up the hold of his ship. When the hold was packed tightly with 150 bodies, there was not even enough room to lie down. A small, sickly child would have died long before the ship reached the other side of the ocean.

BOUGHT: ONE SMALL GIRL

After 10 horrible weeks, the ship landed in Boston. Phillis was taken to the market square with the other African captives to be sold as a household servant. She stood naked and shivering, squinting in the bright summer sunlight, clutching a piece of carpet around herself. Small, skinny, with two missing front teeth, she didn't look like a very promising worker.

But something about the tiny girl appealed to Susanna Wheatley, the wife of a successful tailor. Susanna was looking for a new personal maid. She had a few slaves already, but her maid was getting old, and she wanted someone young and strong. Although this little girl was scrawny, there was something interesting about her face, and Susanna was drawn to her. Her husband, John, paid about £10 for the girl, less than it would cost to buy a silver cream jug. The child was sold cheap because the ship manager doubted she would survive.

The Wheatleys bundled the bewildered little girl into their carriage to take her home. As they left the dockside, Susanna glanced at the ship that had come from Africa. Its name was emblazoned on the side: the *Phillis*. On the spot, she named her new slave after the dreadful vessel. Phillis's last name would be Wheatley, since she belonged to the Wheatleys now.

Black in Boston

To be a black slave in Boston in 1761 meant you worked for your master's family all your life. You were not paid for your work, and you were not taught to read or write. You could go to church, get married, and have children, but your children would be slaves too. You had no choice of whom you worked for or what you did—all was decided for you by your master and mistress.

There were about 1,000 black people in Boston when Phillis arrived there, out of a total city population of 15,000. Of those 1,000 blacks, only 18 were not slaves. Some of the free blacks chose to work as servants; others were entrepreneurs who ran their own businesses. But even the free blacks could not associate freely with white people. In church they were made to sit in their own section at the back or up in the gallery. Although some people in Boston were beginning to question the ethics of slavery, most supported this kind of discrimination.

WRITING ON WALLS

The Wheatleys owned a large red-brick house on busy King Street, in the heart of Boston. John and Susanna were the parents of teenage twins, Nathaniel and Mary. A wealthy tailor, John also owned a store, warehouses, a ship, and several properties in town. The Wheatleys' three other children had all died when they were small, and perhaps this made the family more tender-hearted towards the little stranger. They quickly noticed how intelligent Phillis was. She didn't know a word of English when she arrived, but she learned rapidly and was soon speaking clearly. Mary started reading Phillis the Bible, and since Phillis seemed so interested, Mary also began teaching the child how to read. The girl had some light housekeeping chores to do—dusting, furniture polishing, and serving meals occasionally—but most of her time was taken up with study.

Mary wanted to be a teacher, and she was happy to practice on Phillis. If they had been living in the Southern states, she would have been breaking the law by doing this. It was illegal to teach a slave to read or write in the South. But at a time when even white girls weren't given much education, Phillis found herself in a house where books and learning were considered important.

Whatever result Mary and Susanna might have expected from their teaching experiment, they were astounded by the response from Phillis. She was more than just a bright child. She had a fine mind capable of grasping complicated ideas, and she was fueled by a boundless curiosity. Something deep inside Phillis was stirred by the Christian message of the Bible, too. For the rest of her life, her faith in God sustained her through many troubled times.

Phillis quickly learned to read, and before long she had begun to practice printing letters with a piece of charcoal. She wrote on any surface she could find: rocks, fences, even her bedroom wall. When she discovered what Phillis was doing, Susanna provided the girl with paper, a quill pen, and ink. The other slaves slept in the coach house, but Phillis had her own room in the attic. Susanna gave orders for a fire to be lit in Phillis's bedroom in the cold weather and gave her candles to burn at night.

THE WORLD OF BOOKS

Phillis's desire for knowledge was keen. Mary began teaching her geography, history, math, and English poetry. They moved on to Latin and Greek, and soon the child was translating Ovid (a Roman poet who wrote in Latin) and Homer (a Greek poet) into English.

The Wheatleys had a good library with lots of books for Phillis to read. She went through them as fast as she could and then started borrowing books from the Wheatleys' wealthy friends. She enjoyed reading poetry most of all. Working hard at her studies came naturally to Phillis. For her, learning wasn't work, it was a joy. She advanced so quickly in her grasp of languages and ideas that she was soon better educated than many of the adults around her.

FIRST POEM

Phillis went to church every Sunday at Old South Church. The minister there was the Reverend John Sewall. Phillis enjoyed his sermons and admired him very much. When she was 12, Sewall fell ill and had to be carried to the pulpit in a chair. This stirred her imagination. Phillis expected he would soon die, so she wrote an elegy for him. It began,

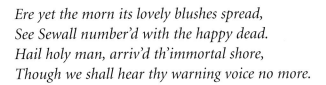

Ere yet the morn its lovely blushes spread,
See Sewall number'd with the happy dead.
Hail holy man, arriv'd th'immortal shore,
Though we shall hear thy warning voice no more.

The poem goes on for 50 lines, depicting the good man's ascent to heaven and offering reflections on death and God. Coming from a 12-year-old girl, it was a remarkably sophisticated piece of writing. Fortunately, Sewall had hidden reserves of strength, and he lived for four more years. Undaunted, Phillis kept working on her poem, revising it several times.

Impressed by Phillis's talent, Susanna encouraged her to write more. Phillis responded with a creative outburst. She wrote poem after poem, composing one whenever she got a good idea. Sometimes she would stay up late at night, working by candlelight, poring over her writing until every line was perfect.

Susanna was so proud of Phillis's accomplishments that she asked her to read poems to friends who dropped by for tea. Phillis reveled in the attention. She liked talking about ideas and books. Soon Susanna was taking the girl with her on social calls, and Phillis and her poetry became a sensation in Boston circles.

BLACK OR WHITE?

It must have been a strange life for Phillis. In the Wheatleys' home she was treated almost as one of the family; she joined them at the dinner table and spent her leisure time with them. She was educated to think and speak like a white person. But when visitors came, the Wheatleys conformed to the social customs of the time and required that Phillis act like a servant, sometimes even serving food at meals.

Susanna's wealthy friends made a great fuss over Phillis, praising her poetry and chatting happily with her. When it came time to drink tea and eat little cakes, however, Phillis was seated at a separate table, set apart from the other ladies by the color of her skin. Yet she was not really comfortable with other black slaves. Susanna discouraged Phillis from associating with them, expecting the servants to treat Phillis as they did other members of the Wheatley family. So, Phillis was caught between two worlds—one white and one black—and had no clearly defined place in either.

A Dead Teacher

The person who taught Phillis the most about writing poetry died 10 years before she was born. Alexander Pope (1688–1744) was a popular English poet and Phillis's favorite. She read his poems again and again, and she learned to write poetry herself by studying his style. Pope always wrote in rhyming couplets (a form in which every two lines rhyme), and Phillis used this same pattern. He wrote clever (and often funny) poems about the follies of human nature, with many references to Greek and Roman mythology and literature. Phillis too made good use of her classical education in her poetry. Some of Pope's poems created vivid pictures of beauty in nature, while others were elegies—sad poems written to honor people who had died. Phillis's first poem was an elegy, and she wrote many more of them throughout her life.

A RISING STAR

When she wrote poetry, though, Phillis was free. Her talent lifted her to a place where she had a voice of her own. In her poems she could explore her feelings and express her opinions. Her writing covered many subjects from the world around her; she was always curious about new situations, people, and issues. She drew inspiration from the heady political climate of the time (the colony was on the verge of revolution) and from religious themes. Phillis had a wonderful imagination; she also had the language skills to create a poetic structure that would get her ideas across to readers.

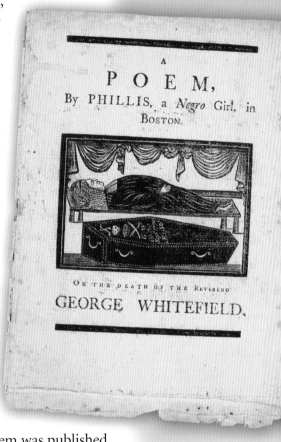

One evening at dinner, when Phillis was 14 years old, she heard the thrilling tale of a near shipwreck from two visitors, Mr. Hussey and Mr. Coffin. That night she wrote a poem about it, called "On Mssrs. Hussey and Coffin." Susanna submitted it to a local newspaper, the *Newport Mercury*, and on December 21, 1767, the poem was published.

Several more of Phillis's poems appeared in print over the next few years. She must have been very pleased to see that all her hard work was appreciated. When a charismatic English preacher, the Reverend George Whitefield, died suddenly from a stroke, Phillis put quill pen to paper to pay tribute to him. Phillis had heard Whitefield speak while he was on an American tour. He preached that people of all colors were equal in the eyes of God. Her elegy made an impact on both sides of the Atlantic. It appeared in more than a dozen newspapers in New York, Boston, and Pennsylvania and was circulated in London, England, where Whitefield had a huge following.

PROVE IT!

Now that Phillis was receiving so much acclaim, Susanna set out to get a book of her poems published in America. In those days, a writer had to collect the names of subscribers who would pay for his or her book in advance. A book of 200 pages needed 300 subscribers to go ahead. But the American public was not ready to invest in a book written by a slave, no matter how famous she was.

There was another problem: because of the prejudice of the time, many people didn't believe that Phillis had written the poems. They suspected that either Susanna or Mary was the real author.

War is Brewing

Phillis Wheatley lived in an exciting time and place. Boston was at the heart of the American Revolution. The Stamp Act Riot, the Boston Massacre, and the Boston Tea Party all took place almost literally outside her front door.

The Wheatleys' house on King Street was only one block from Faneuil Hall, where all the town meetings took place. Any public demonstration usually erupted into King Street. In August 1765, Boston merchants and townspeople took to the streets, shouting and marching against the Stamp Act—a new tax imposed by the British on many daily transactions, which took money from the colonists nearly every time they did business. The unpopular act would be repealed the following year by King George III, but tensions remained high, and the King sent English soldiers to patrol the streets of Boston in a show of force. In 1770, a scuffle between a soldier and a citizen turned ugly. The soldiers started firing their guns, and five colonists were killed just a few blocks from the Wheatleys' house. The event became known as the Boston Massacre.

In 1772, Susanna arranged for Phillis to take a special test. Eighteen men gathered (perhaps in the public meeting rooms at Faneuil Hall) to ask the young writer questions about her education. The examiners included the governor of Massachusetts and the lieutenant governor, as well as other respected public figures. They sat in a semicircle, and Phillis stood in front of them.

Phillis never wrote about how she felt that day, but it is easy to imagine she was pretty nervous. Although she was confident about her writing and accustomed to discussing ideas, she was only 19, and she had to think fast and stay calm in order to prove herself.

There is no record of what the men asked her. Phillis had been thoroughly educated in classical literature; they may have asked her about that, or tested her knowledge of Greek, Latin, history, or geography. Whatever they asked her, she must have given the right answers—the examiners declared themselves completely satisfied and signed a declaration stating that Phillis was qualified to write her poems.

In 1773, Bostonians reacted angrily to a tax that forced them to buy British tea at high prices. Seven thousand townspeople gathered at Old South Church, where Phillis attended services. The crowd marched down to the docks and dumped 342 chests of tea into the water in protest. The demonstration was instantly christened the Boston Tea Party.

Phillis carefully observed what was going on around her, and many of her poems were inspired by the people and events in the revolutionary struggle against England.

A CELEBRITY'S WELCOME

One of Rev. George Whitefield's patrons had been the Countess Selina of Huntingdon, a close friend of Susanna Wheatley. When Phillis was 20, the countess arranged to publish a collection of her poetry in England. Susanna suggested that Phillis sail to London with Mary's twin brother, Nathaniel, who was going over on business. Every winter Phillis suffered terribly with her asthma in the icy Boston climate. Susanna hoped the sea voyage and change of air would improve the young woman's health.

Phillis, as a fond goodbye to Mrs. Wheatley, wrote a poem called "A Farewell to America." Once in England, though, she had little time for homesickness. Everyone wanted to meet her: writers, poets, society ladies, dukes, lords—even the King. She was caught up in a whirlwind of sightseeing, visiting, and parties, all the while working with her publisher to prepare her poems for printing. The Earl of Dartmouth, hearing of Phillis's devotion to Alexander Pope, gave her enough money to buy the poet's complete works. They were the first books Phillis ever owned.

Phillis's trip was cut short by an urgent letter from Boston: Susanna was very sick. Dreadfully worried, Phillis boarded the

In Her Own Words

"In every Breast, God has implanted a Principle which we call Love of Freedom; it is impatient of Oppression, and pants for Deliverance."

—from a letter to Rev. Samson Occom, February 11, 1774, after Phillis gained her freedom from slavery

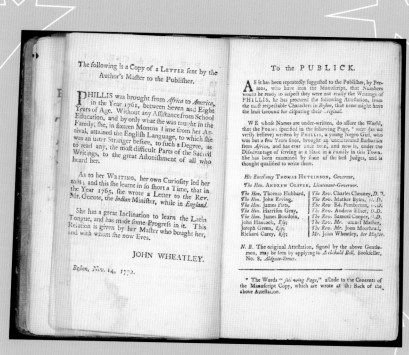

The following is a Copy of a LETTER sent by the Author's Master to the Publisher.

PHILLIS was brought from *Africa* to *America*, in the Year 1761, between Seven and Eight Years of Age. Without any Assistance from School Education, and by only what she was taught in the Family, she, in sixteen Months Time from her Arrival, attained the English Language, to which she was an utter Stranger before, to such a Degree, as to read any, the most difficult Parts of the Sacred Writings, to the great Astonishment of all who heard her.

As to her WRITING, her own Curiosity led her to it; and this she learnt in so short a Time, that in the Year 1765, she wrote a Letter to the Rev. Mr. OCCOM, the *Indian* Minister, while in *England*.

She has a great Inclination to learn the Latin Tongue, and has made some Progress in it. This Relation is given by her Master who bought her, and with whom she now lives.

JOHN WHEATLEY.

Boston, Nov. 14, 1772.

To the PUBLICK.

AS it has been repeatedly suggested to the Publisher, by Persons, who have seen the Manuscript, that Numbers would be ready to suspect they were not really the Writings of PHILLIS, he has procured the following Attestation, from the most respectable Characters in *Boston*, that none might have the least Ground for disputing their Original.

WE whose Names are under-written, do assure the World, that the POEMS specified in the following Page, * were (as we verily believe) written by PHILLIS, a young Negro Girl, who was but a few Years since, brought an uncultivated Barbarian from *Africa*, and has ever since been, and now is, under the Disadvantage of serving as a Slave in a Family in this Town. She has been examined by some of the best Judges, and is thought qualified to write them.

His Excellency THOMAS HUTCHINSON, *Governor,*
The Hon. ANDREW OLIVER, *Lieutenant-Governor.*

The Hon. Thomas Hubbard, | *The Rev.* Charles Chauncy, *D. D.*
The Hon. John Erving, | *The Rev.* Mather Byles, *D. D.*
The Hon. James Pitts, | *The Rev.* Ed. Pemberton, *D. D.*
The Hon. Harrison Gray, | *The Rev.* Andrew Eliot, *D. D.*
The Hon. James Bowdoin, | *The Rev.* Samuel Cooper, *D. D.*
John Hancock, *Esq;* | *The Rev. Mr.* Samuel Mather,
Joseph Green, *Esq;* | *The Rev. Mr.* John Moorhead,
Richard Carey, *Esq;* | *Mr.* John Wheatley, *her Master.*

N. B. The original Attestation, signed by the above Gentlemen, may be seen by applying to *Archibald Bell*, Bookseller, No. 8, *Aldgate-Street.*

_____

* The Words "*following Page,*" allude to the Contents of the Manuscript Copy, which are wrote at the Back of the above Attestation.

Phillis Wheatley's book of poems included a brief introduction by her master, followed by a declaration from the Boston dignitaries who examined her.

first ship bound for home. Upon her return, she found Susanna to be deathly ill but still clinging to life. Phillis did her best to care for her mistress over the next few months.

MAKING HISTORY

"*POEMS—On various subjects—Religious and Moral* by Phillis Wheatley, a Negro girl" was published in England in 1773. The first thing readers saw when they opened the book was Phillis's portrait, which had been engraved by a black slave in Boston who was also an artist, Scipio Moorhead. In the picture, Phillis sits with a quill pen in hand, writing a poem. Following this came a note from John Wheatley about how Phillis had learned to read and write. Then came a declaration from the Boston dignitaries who had tested Phillis. Finally came the poems themselves—39 of them.

It is difficult to understand today just how extraordinary the publication of Phillis's book was. Not only was she the first African-American slave to publish a book, but she was also only the third woman in the American colonies to publish a book of poetry.

FREEDOM

The British public responded warmly to Phillis's book, and most critics approved. But a few raised the question of her enslavement: why did this young woman, so championed by her Boston friends, still have the status of a slave?

In 1774, Susanna and John Wheatley gave Phillis a present. A set of official documents, called manumission papers, set Phillis free at the age of 21.

Phillis was very happy. In a letter to Rev. Samson Occom, a minister friend, she said that everyone is born with a desire for freedom. How could Americans say they believed in liberty, she asked, and yet keep blacks enslaved? In a poem dedicated to the Earl of Dartmouth, Phillis wrote: "I, young in life, by seeming cruel fate / Was snatch'd from *Afric*'s fancy'd happy seat." The poem concluded, "And can I then but pray / Others may never feel tyrannic sway."

WHAT HAPPENED NEXT

Susanna Wheatley died soon after she granted Phillis her freedom. Phillis was heartbroken to lose her dear friend. But Susanna had lived long enough to see Phillis's book of poetry being sold in the American colonies. After its great success in England, 300 copies arrived in Boston in January 1774.

Phillis stayed with John Wheatley for a while, then moved in with Mary and her husband and children in Providence, Rhode Island. It had become dangerous to live in Boston. Four thousand English soldiers had arrived, taking over many buildings. The Wheatleys' house was blown up by a bomb, and their church was used as a pigsty.

By April 1775, England and the American colonies were at war. Phillis wrote a poem to inspire the American commander in chief, George Washington, and he asked to meet her when he visited Boston. Although there were businessmen and politicians lined up to see him, Washington spent 30 minutes talking to the writer he so admired.

There were some sad losses in store for Phillis, however. John Wheatley and Mary Wheatley both died in 1778, and John had made no provision for Phillis in his will. Phillis tried to sell more of her books, and she worked on another volume of poetry. She couldn't raise the money to publish it, though. She still suffered from asthma and her health was poor.

A few weeks after John Wheatley's death, Phillis married a free black man, John Peters, who had various occupations, including barber, baker, lawyer, and doctor. He suffered from financial problems, though, and sadly the couple had two babies who did not live long. In 1784, John Peters was sent to debtors' prison. Phillis found a job washing sheets in a boardinghouse. But she wasn't strong enough for this kind of physical labor, and she soon fell ill. She died on December 5, 1784, at the age of 31. Her third child, a sickly little baby, died a few hours later. No one knows where Phillis and her baby were buried.

In a poem published four months before her death, Phillis speaks to parents whose baby son has died, trying to console them

Phillis Wheatley Lives On

Phillis Wheatley had no way of knowing how famous she would eventually become. Her life and her accomplishments have inspired generations of African-Americans. Countless institutions across the United States have been named after her: community centers, hospitals, libraries, schools—even girls' baseball teams.

There has been some controversy about Phillis's fame because some say she betrayed other black people by adopting the opinions and attitudes of the white society she lived in. However, Phillis had no choice but to take on the culture and language of her owners. Within the very restricted confines of her life as a slave, she went further than anyone would have dreamed possible.

with the thought that their baby is in heaven and his suffering is over. Perhaps she took some comfort in this idea since her own life had become so difficult. As a devout Christian, she believed that when she died she would be with God, along with her children and friends.

SPEND MORE TIME WITH PHILLIS

Phillis Wheatley's poetry is sometimes hard for the modern reader to understand. Its style seems old-fashioned, and it includes many religious and classical references most of us are not familiar with today. Excerpts from her poems can be found on websites and in books about her life.

A Voice of Her Own: The Story of Phillis Wheatley, Slave Poet
by Kathryn Lasky
Phillis and her years in Boston come alive in this book, which is beautifully illustrated by Paul Lee.

Phillis Wheatley, Poet by Merle Richmond (American Women of Achievement Series)
Merle Richmond has written a fascinating book about Phillis's life. Richly illustrated with material from the time period, the book offers an intriguing look at the issue of slavery and the social upheaval wrought by the American Revolution.

THE WALKING POLYGLOT

Maria Gaetana Agnesi

1718–1799

*M*aria stood frozen in the doorway to the grand ballroom, clutching her little sister's hand tightly. The room was filled with glittering candlelight and swirling colors. The best of Milan society in 1727 were all enjoying themselves at the elegant party arranged by her father, Pietro Agnesi. The noise of laughing and chattering grown-ups rose up all around her, along with the thick smell of perfumes and warm bodies. Her head throbbed and she felt a wave of dizziness. Then her father's smiling face swam into view, beckoning her forward. Silence fell as the girls took a few steps into the room. Theresa sat down at the harpsichord while Maria stood beside her, trembling.

"Bonsoir, Buenas tardes, Guten Abend," she began. "Good evening, ladies and gentlemen. I will now present a speech in Latin about why it is important to educate women, and then my sister will play for you."

Her audience listened appreciatively as the nine-year-old girl gave her talk in clear, correct Latin. As she spoke, she gradually stopped shaking and her voice grew stronger. But Maria hated the attention and was happy when it was over. Her father insisted that his young daughters appear at these gatherings, showing off their marvelous skills and their excellent education. But Maria would have preferred to be alone in her room, reading.

Even though she dreaded the public performances, Maria knew she was fortunate to have a father who believed that girls should be educated. Most girls in Italy in the 1720s didn't even learn to read, and when rich families sent their daughters away to convents to be

$$y = \frac{8a^3}{x^2 + 4a^2}$$

educated, they usually studied household management, etiquette (good manners), and religion.

Maria Agnesi made her mark in a man's world as a brilliant mathematician.

But attitudes towards women and education were changing all over Europe in the 18th century. A few Italian girls were taught academic subjects, just like their brothers, and some went to university lectures. Pietro Agnesi, a wealthy man whose family had made its fortune selling fine silks, provided his daughters and sons with the best tutors in Milan.

From the time she was very small, Maria displayed a remarkable ability to learn languages. She spoke French as well as Italian by the age of five, and by the time she reached 13 she was fluent in at least five more languages: Greek, Hebrew, Latin, German, and Spanish. People called her the Walking Polyglot (a polyglot is someone who speaks many languages) and the Oracle of the Seven Tongues.

In Her Own Words

For if at any time there can be an excuse for the rashness of a Woman who ventures to aspire to the subtleties of a science which knows no bounds, not even those of infinity itself, it certainly should be at this glorious period, in which a Woman reigns ... Indeed, I am fully convinced that in this age ... every Woman ought to exert herself and endeavor to promote the glory of her sex and to contribute her utmost.

—from Maria Agnesi's math textbook, which she dedicated to Empress Maria Theresa of Austria, the most powerful woman in Europe at the time

Maria excelled at everything else she studied too, with particular skills in mathematics and philosophy. Her younger sister Theresa was a musical prodigy, playing the harpsichord (a form of small piano), singing, and composing.

Pietro was so proud of his daughters that he organized entertainment evenings to showcase their talent. Neighbors, friends, and visiting nobility dressed up in their fanciest clothes and came to the Agnesi mansion. The luxurious rooms sparkled with jewels and sophisticated conversation. Theresa played splendidly and Maria gave learned talks about various subjects; she could debate almost any topic with the distinguished guests, answering them in the language of their choice. Everyone "oohed" and "ahhhed" in admiration of the exceptional young girls.

When Maria was 14, her mother died giving birth to her eighth baby. Maria had to take over running the household and teaching the younger children, as well as attending to her own studies. The stress caused her to have seizures and fainting spells. She begged her father to excuse her from the public lectures, but he refused. Pietro remarried twice, and eventually Maria had 20 brothers and sisters. What she really wanted was to become a nun and help the poor, but her father insisted she stay at home and tutor her little brothers and sisters.

When Maria grew up, she published two important books. The first, which appeared when she was 20, was a collection of 191 essays called *Philosophical Propositions*, based on her public talks. It took her 10 years to produce her second book, *Analytical Institutions*, a wonderfully clear textbook in two volumes that explored the major mathematical concepts of the time. This was the first book published by a woman about math, and it proved that a woman could think as brilliantly as a man. The text drew praise from many academics. The Pope was so impressed that he appointed Maria an honorary professor of mathematics and philosophy at the University of Bologna.

Maria never took up the post. It was not in her nature to pursue a public career, and her father was very ill. He died in 1752, when Maria was 34. From then on, Maria devoted her life to God. She spent her inheritance on setting up a home for old people, where she took on the position of director. She died there at the age of 81.

SPEND MORE TIME WITH MARIA

Many people have never heard of Maria Agnesi, but if they've studied math they may have come across something called the Witch of Agnesi, a mathematical formula. An Englishman named John Colson made a mistake when he was translating Maria's book into English. Maria explained a formula used to describe a curved line. She called the formula *la versiera*, which means "a curved rope." Colson mistook that word for the Italian word *l'aversiera*, which refers to a witch or she-devil. Why he would think a curved line would be called a witch is a mystery, but somehow the word stuck. The formula has been called the Witch of Agnesi ever since.

This is what the Witch of Agnesi looks like:

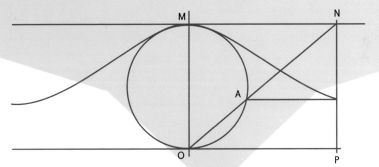

To see a moving illustration of how the calculation for the Witch of Agnesi makes a curve, go to this website: http://mathworld.wolfram.com/WitchofAgnesi.html. The curve grows as you watch.

Clara Schumann

1819–1896

"**G**ive it back!" howled Alvin, throwing himself on his brother. "It's mine, give it back!"

Gustav laughed, squirming under Alvin's weight. "It's not yours! I won him fair and square!"

"You cheated," roared Alvin, pulling hard on Gustav's hair.

"Oww!" screamed Gustav, but his fist stayed tightly curled around the toy soldier. The boys rolled over and over and bumped up against the piano leg.

Clara turned the page and kept playing. She had a peaceful smile on her lips and a faraway look in her eyes. She didn't see the parlor with its stuffed sofa and straight-backed chairs, or the window that looked out into the gray street where the November rain was pouring down. She was playing the first movement of Mozart's Piano Sonata in A, one of her favorite pieces. The sonata started slowly, with a falling rhythm that was infinitely sad, infinitely beautiful. The boys kept yelling at each other, but she didn't hear them. She heard only the notes she was playing, as they lifted her into a world of sound far beyond her squabbling brothers and her demanding father, a place where Clara and Mozart and the sweet melody all danced together.

Clara hadn't been allowed to play the Mozart piece for seven days, two hours, and 25 minutes. That was how long it had been since her father had flown into a violent rage during her morning lesson and locked her music away in a suitcase. A week before his temper tantrum, she had performed in public for the first time. It had been so thrilling to play in front of all those people, wearing her lovely new silk dress with the ruffles. The applause and the cheering had risen like a wave, filling her with a brimming joy she had never felt before.

Her father had been so pleased with what the critics wrote about her. He had walked up and down, rubbing his hands together and laughing, telling her this was just the beginning—he and Clara would soon show the world what a brilliant teacher he was.

But a few days later Clara had forgotten to play a repeat in a new piece of music. Her father started screaming at her, then tore the music into little shreds and threw them up in the air. "You are lazy and disobedient, you wretched girl! After all I've done to help you, you can't even pay attention! No more lessons for you until you change your stubborn ways. You'll be playing nothing but scales until you prove to me you're sorry."

He kept on shouting, waving his arms around his head and looming over her like a big hungry bear. Clara sat with tears streaming down her face, not daring to move or utter a single word. She had apologized every day since, but her father had not relented, and so she was stuck with playing endless scales and exercises. But today, for no apparent reason, he had finally given in and returned her music.

Clara always tried to watch her father for signs of a bad mood, but it wasn't much use. He could be smiling one minute and shouting the next. When he was pleased, he sat beside her as she played and they were transported by the swirling, sweeping music. Then she felt closer to him than to anyone else on earth. His blue eyes twinkled and his stern expression melted into smiles.

But when he got angry, her father erupted into a raging demon. He hit Alvin and Gustav sometimes. He'd knock their heads together and twist their arms. But he never struck Clara. He didn't need to. The worst thing he could do to her was to take away her music. It was like food for her, like water, or even the air she breathed. She couldn't live without it. Only when she was in that magical world did she feel truly alive, truly herself.

THE SILENT CHILD

People thought Clara Wieck was deaf. She was nearly five and yet she couldn't talk. The tiny girl with the huge blue eyes didn't seem to understand what anyone said to her. But her parents, Frederick and Marianne Wieck, didn't have much time to worry about it because they were arguing so much.

Clara's mother had just had her fifth baby, and she had come to a terrible decision: to leave her husband. In 1824 in Leipzig, Germany, a woman had no rights in a divorce. The husband usually kept the children and the property. Frederick Wieck was so furious with his wife that he took custody of all the children, including the new baby. Soon he fired Clara's nanny because he thought she sided with Marianne.

Clara was left without the two women who had loved her all her life. But Frederick Wieck had big plans for his silent little daughter. Shortly after her fifth birthday, he sat Clara down at the piano, her legs dangling high above the floor. Frederick began to play a dance he had composed especially for her. It was a merry, simple tune, and the child smiled as she listened. He played it again, and her eyes fastened on his fingers as they moved across the keys. Then he picked up her hands and placed them gently on the keys. The child began to play, imitating her father's movements.

It was the beginning of a new life for both of them. Clara loved sitting with her big, strong father at the piano and playing the pretty songs he made up. He didn't expect her to talk; all she had to do was follow his fingers and then do the same movements with hers. Far from being deaf, Clara had an astonishing ear for music. Sometimes she only had to hear a tune once and she could play it perfectly.

Frederick began a daily program of piano lessons, and Clara responded with joy, diligently practicing the tunes her father taught her. She wanted to please him, so she always did her best. She even began to talk—slowly at first, but gradually adding more words.

Magnificent Mozart

Wolfgang Amadeus Mozart (1756–1791), one of the world's greatest composers, is history's most famous child prodigy, probably because his genius was so startling—he began playing the harpsichord when he was three and had composed his first music by the time he was five. Like Clara, Mozart was taught by his father and groomed to be a virtuoso from a very young age. He gave his first public performance when he was six, and went on to an almost continuous tour of the royal courts of Europe throughout his childhood. Mozart's fame and the money he made for his father inspired many proud parents to try to mold their musical children into prodigies. Several well-known composers in the 19th century began their careers as children, including Felix and Fanny Mendelssohn (see page 54), Franz Liszt, and Frédéric Chopin.

A DOOMED MARRIAGE

Frederick Wieck had grown up in a family without much money. He hated being poor, and he was determined to make his way in the world and prove himself. After graduating from university, he got a job as a private tutor in a rich family's house. The serious-minded, conscientious young man was good at his work. He studied the latest theories in education and applied them to his pupils.

But although Frederick was a successful tutor, he knew it was a dead-end career. When he was 30, he took a big risk: borrowing some money from a friend, he opened a piano store in the music-friendly city of Leipzig. His shop was conveniently located just a few steps from the main square, and he took in piano pupils. Frederick's own musical training had been haphazard. What he really had going for him was an extreme self-confidence. His students were impressed with his obvious intelligence and his astute teaching methods, and soon Frederick was one of the most respected piano teachers in the city.

To be really famous, though, Frederick needed an outstanding pupil. When he started teaching Marianne Tromlitz, an accomplished young pianist with a lovely singing voice, he believed he had found his star. High-spirited, attractive, and just 19, Marianne came from a musical family. Her grandfather was a famous flutist, composer, and teacher. Frederick knew that Marianne's success could raise both his status as a teacher and his income. He asked her to marry him, and she agreed.

Marianne set out to be everything Frederick wanted her to be. She performed in public regularly, singing solos and playing the piano at concerts; she ran the house and the servants; she taught pupils advanced piano and voice; and she had five children, two of whom died as infants. But her new husband had high standards and little patience. He criticized Marianne, demanding she do more.

Clara's father, Frederick, was a stern and demanding taskmaster who controlled every aspect of his daughter's education and career.

At age eight Clara was small for her age, but she played the piano with astonishing strength.

Finally Marianne had had enough ill treatment. Within a year of divorcing Frederick, she married again and moved to Berlin. From then on, Clara and her brothers would have only brief visits with their mother.

CREATING A STAR

Clara's father had chosen her name, which means "brilliance" or "shining." Even when she was a baby, he had high hopes for his child. Now that his wife was gone, Frederick needed another accomplished pupil to bring him fame and fortune. With her extraordinary aptitude for music, little Clara would be the ideal subject to illustrate his teaching methods. He would shape her

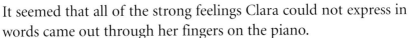

huge talent to produce the most celebrated pianist in Europe.

Clara's progress at the piano was astounding. Like all prodigies, she had abilities far beyond her age, and she worked hard. Everything fit together so perfectly in music, with a mathematical precision that she understood instinctively. It seemed that all of the strong feelings Clara could not express in words came out through her fingers on the piano.

Unlike some parents of child musicians, Frederick didn't believe in long hours of practice. Clara had a one-hour piano lesson and two hours of practice every day, a couple of hours studying with a tutor, and then a long walk in the fresh air. Aside from her brothers, she had no other children to play with, and no dolls or toys. But from the time she was six, Frederick took her to the theater, concerts, and the opera. As she grew up, her father arranged for Clara to have musical instruction from the best teachers available. She learned music theory, harmony, counterpoint, composition, singing, and violin.

In the 1820s, Leipzig was a city echoing with music—a perfect place for Clara to pursue her musical education. Nearly every parlor had a piano, and people amused themselves by gathering with friends to play instruments and sing. Along with his excellent reputation as a teacher, Frederick was known for his sense of humor and his endless enthusiasm for good music. The finest of the local musicians came to his musical evenings, to chat and play their new pieces.

Clara started playing for her father's friends when she was six. The grown-ups gave her a rousing welcome. They were entranced with this tiny musician who sat down so confidently and played so skillfully. Clara loved their attention, and the applause and cheers made her feel warm and happy. But Frederick's plans for Clara went far beyond playing for his friends. He wanted her to give concerts all over Europe. His intention was to create a virtuoso, a musician

The public square and marketplace in Leipzig, the musical city where Clara grew up.

with such dazzling technique that she would far outshine other pianists. He kept his talented daughter to a disciplined schedule of lessons and practice.

STEPPING INTO THE SPOTLIGHT

When Clara was nine, Frederick married a woman named Clementine. Clara may have been concerned at first that her new stepmother would claim her father's time, but she needn't have worried. For Frederick, Clara always came first: before Alvin and Gustav, before Clementine, and before the new babies who would arrive over the next few years. The whole household revolved around Clara and her career—her piano, her concerts, her clothes.

This was the year that Frederick decided his daughter was ready for her public debut. He arranged for her to play at the Gewandhaus, a famous Leipzig concert hall. The Wieck household was in a state of excitement for weeks beforehand, and Clara's father bought her a beautiful silk dress to wear for the concert. On October 28, 1828, Clara appeared onstage for the first time, playing a duet with another student. She performed brilliantly, and the audience was smitten.

Frederick took Clara to the city of Dresden for a month in the spring of 1830 to give a series of private concerts in the luxurious homes and palaces of aristocrats. She was an instant success. Ladies showered her with presents of jewelry and came to fix her hair. Clara played music by well-known composers—Bach, Mozart, and Beethoven—as well as her own compositions. It was the custom for pianists to play some of their own work at each performance, and Clara had been composing since the age of nine.

Frederick was very pleased with his daughter's growing popularity and her progress as a musician. All was going according to plan. His next move was to arrange her solo debut at the Gewandhaus, in November 1830. Once again, the audience and the critics raved about her.

The Strength of Six Boys

People were always surprised by the power of Clara's playing. Until she reached her teens, she was a very small, skinny girl. She looked like a gust of wind would knock her over. But when she sat down at the piano, she played with a muscular intensity that was quite startling. When the writer Johann Wolfgang Goethe heard her play at age 12, he declared, "She plays with as much strength as six boys."

The two other most accomplished virtuosos in Clara's time were both male: Franz Liszt (piano) and Niccolò Paganini (violin). But neither Clara nor her father ever let her gender stand in the way of her success. Her father believed she could accomplish anything. Her talent, skillful playing, determination, and hard work ensured that she went far beyond society's usual expectations for a woman.

As an adult, Clara taught for many years at a musical conservatory in Frankfurt. The director was quoted as saying, "With the exception of Madame Schumann there is no woman and there will not be any women employed in the Conservatory. As for Madame Schumann, I count her as a man." Although it seems insulting to us today, at the time this was considered a great compliment. There is no record of how Clara felt about it.

THE BUMPY ROAD TO PARIS

Now it was time to build on Clara's success. Frederick arranged a seven-month tour of Europe for spring 1831. They were to end up in Paris, the continent's hub of music, culture, and fashion. The two set off together, traveling in cold coaches with hard seats that bumped along the roads for hours. They stayed in modest hotels, ate irregular meals, and packed in as many performances as possible.

This first tour was the model for all those that came afterwards. Frederick was a born hustler—he made the most of his contacts and introductions to influential people, promoting Clara at every opportunity. He controlled all the arrangements for her concerts: booking the halls, taking care of advertising, fixing the piano if necessary, collecting money at the door, and sometimes selling signed photographs of his daughter at the end of the evening.

Everywhere they went, the crowds and the critics loved Clara. What people found so amazing was the contrast between her age and the artistry she demonstrated. Not only did she play with a level of technical skill that surpassed many adult performers, but she exhibited an emotional maturity and understanding in her music that went far beyond her years. Clara would blend these qualities in her performances all her life: superb technique coupled with intense emotion.

Frederick wrote letters to his wife, Clementine, complaining about life on the road, but Clara had a wonderful time. Every night when she sat down at the piano in front of a rapt audience, she entered a world much bigger than that of bumpy roads and uncomfortable hotels. Concertgoers would hang on every note she played, then react with thunderous applause. For Clara, it was heaven.

"Dad Writes My Diary"

Today a person's diary is supposed to be personal and private. But Clara's father not only read her diary, he often wrote in it himself, pretending to be her. Frederick used the diary as another way of controlling his daughter. He started it for her when Clara was seven, so that she could practice her handwriting while making a record of daily events. But often Frederick wrote what he thought she should be thinking and feeling. Clara could never use the diary to write about anything secret, and she had to be careful not to include anything that would annoy her father.

A MUSICAL FRIEND

One of the regulars at Clara's father's musical gatherings was a dark-haired, handsome 18-year-old student named Robert Schumann. Robert was supposed to be studying law in Leipzig, but he was always goofing off from his studies and going along to the Wiecks' house to soak up the musical atmosphere, playing duets with Clara and reading books from their well-stocked library. Robert was a good piano player, but his real strength was his skill at improvisation. He could sit at the piano and make up the music as he went along, enchanting his audience with imaginative variations on a musical theme.

When he turned 20, Robert Schumann begged his mother to let him give up law and study piano with Frederick instead. His mother wrote to Frederick to ask his advice. She wasn't sure if Robert had the talent or the ambition to be a successful musician. Frederick told Mrs. Schumann that Robert could develop his talent if he settled down to a strict regimen of practice and lessons. Overjoyed, Robert moved in with the Wiecks.

Robert brought a welcome sense of fun to the serious household. He played games with Clara and her brothers, told them stories, and dressed up as a ghost to scare them. He organized standing-on-one-leg contests with Gustav and Alvin, seeing who could last the longest. There hadn't been much of this kind of fooling around in the Wieck family, and they all loved him.

Especially Clara. She was 11 by now, and she felt as if she had acquired an instant older brother. Robert grew very fond of her, too. He would sometimes get frustrated when he heard Clara practicing—she played so much better than he did. But they shared a keen love of music and could play and talk about music together for hours. They helped each other with problems of composition, and they dedicated pieces to each other.

It gradually became clear that Robert's gift was as a composer, not a piano player. In those days, the only way to publicize your music was to have it played by fellow musicians. Clara's sensitive interpretations of his pieces would help to build his reputation as one of Europe's most exciting new composers.

Musical Soul Mates

When Clara was 11, she wrote a musical piece called "Romance" (Opus 3) and dedicated it to Robert Schumann. "Opus 3" meant it was her third published composition. It started with a sweet, simple melody and continued with seven variations of the tune. Robert composed a piece called "Impromptus" (Opus 5), based on the same melody. Although Clara was still a child and Robert a young man of 20, their lifelong musical conversation had begun.

LOVE AND LETTERS

Robert admired Frederick as a teacher, but he found the older man's rages unsettling, and he was shocked at how Frederick bullied and humiliated his sons. One day Robert watched as Frederick threw Alvin to the ground and pulled his hair, shouting at him all

Robert Schumann was playful, handsome, and a brilliantly original composer.

the while. The reason? Alvin had played something badly on the violin. What stunned Robert about this whole scene was Clara's reaction: she just smiled, sat down at the piano, and began to play. For an outsider like Robert, the Wiecks all seemed a bit crazy.

Crazy or not, by the time Clara was 16 the friendship between her and Robert had blossomed into love. It was inevitable: they were two passionate musicians living under the same roof and sharing their delight in music day after day. They tried to keep their feelings for each other secret, but Frederick eventually found out. Predictably, he was furious. He had spent years training Clara and shaping her career, and he didn't want her money and fame to be snatched from him. He forbade them to see each other, threatening to kill Robert if he disobeyed. Then he whisked Clara away on a prolonged concert tour.

Clara and Robert stayed in touch by secretly writing each other long letters. Sympathetic friends smuggled their correspondence back and forth. When Clara turned 18, Robert wrote to her father asking to marry her. Frederick refused. He shouted that he would disown Clara if she married Robert, and he began to say terrible things about Robert in public. According to the laws of the time, Clara had to have both her parents' permission to marry. It was very difficult for the two lovers to stay hopeful when they had so much against them. They each struggled with despair and doubt during their enforced separation, which was to last several years.

Classical or Romantic?

Clara and Robert Schumann were Romantic musicians—not because they were in love, but because they were part of an exhilarating new trend in the 19th century called Romanticism. The most famous composers of the 18th century (Bach, Mozart, and Haydn) all wrote Classical music: it followed careful rules of harmony and composition. But starting with Beethoven, composers let their imagination take them in whatever direction it wanted to go. The result was lyrical music with many variations on a central theme.

Beethoven, Robert Schumann, Brahms, and many other innovative musicians broke loose from the highly structured forms of Classical music to express themselves more fully. The Classical style represented order, reason, and logic; Romanticism was fueled by emotion, nature, and old, heroic stories. The Romantic movement influenced music, art, literature, dance, philosophy, and architecture for more than a hundred years.

TRIUMPH IN VIENNA

Despite the turbulence in Clara's personal life, she was playing more magnificently than ever. Frederick had arranged a long stay in Vienna, where the people were stunned by her electric performances. Clara's fans stormed the box office, fighting for seats. The police had to be called to calm the riot. Everyone raved about the young virtuoso—music critics adored her, aristocrats asked her to dinner, musicians sang her praises. Clara was so popular that the Viennese bakers created a dessert named after her: *torte à la Wieck*. The rich confection was made up of layers of pastry and whipped cream, topped with a flourish of rosettes made of icing.

The Emperor of Austria, Ferdinand I, was intrigued by all the fuss. He asked Clara to play for him, and was so delighted with her performance that he awarded her a title: Royal and Imperial Chamber Virtuoso. This was a great honor for anyone, but exceptional for such a young woman.

Clara worked hard in Vienna. Always on display, she had to play brilliantly at her concerts and then go on to parties and socialize with high society. Her confidence in herself grew. She was famous throughout Europe now, and she knew her father's iron rule could not last forever.

Mr. All-for-Money

Robert Schumann made up a nickname for Frederick when he lived with the Wiecks: Meister Allesgeld (Mr. All-for-Money). Although he was raking in the money from Clara's concerts, Frederick kept most of it for himself and gave her only a small allowance for candy and postage stamps. When she left him to get married, Clara had to sue her father to get back some of what she had earned as a child performer. Frederick believed that all the money should belong to him, since he had worked so hard to build her career.

INDEPENDENCE

After Clara's triumph in Vienna, Frederick sent her off on a tour to Paris by herself, thinking she would be lost without him to make all the arrangements. But Clara had learned a lot during her long years of touring with her father, and she managed everything beautifully.

Still, it took five years from the time of their first kiss for Robert Schumann and Clara to overcome the obstacles Frederick put in their path. They went to court to get permission to marry, and Robert sued Frederick for the lies he had spread about him. In the midst of the turmoil Clara grew close to her mother again, and she lived with Marianne for a few years after her father locked her out of the house.

Finally, just after Clara's 21st birthday, she married Robert, leaving her father and her childhood behind.

WHAT HAPPENED NEXT

Clara continued with her career after her marriage. It wasn't easy. She loved going on tour—the excitement of new people and places, the thrill of performing—but Robert hated it. He much preferred to stay at home and write music. They didn't like being apart, but their lives grew ever more complicated. Over time they had eight children, all of whom needed nannies and schools and ongoing attention.

Robert and Clara both took on students. Robert accepted a couple of jobs as a musical director, but he had trouble keeping them. At times he suffered from depression so severe that he could barely speak. Clara covered for him again and again, interpreting his wishes to orchestras or choral groups. It was also up to Clara to handle all the practical household chores.

While Clara was pregnant with her eighth child, Robert tried to kill himself by jumping into a river. He was sent to a mental hospital. The doctors there thought it would be better if Clara didn't see him, so she stayed away. It was a very hard time for her. She loved Robert deeply but knew she could no longer help him.

Clara's strength of character and her passion for music carried her through her long career and many personal tragedies.

She kept touring and playing for audiences, seeking solace in her music. Another great comfort to her at this time was her friend Johannes Brahms, a young composer. He helped Clara with the children and the household accounts and offered her companionship.

After two years in hospital, Robert Schumann grew very ill. As he lay near death, the doctors finally allowed Clara to come to say goodbye. Robert died at the age of 46, making Clara a widow at just 37 years old. It was a tragic loss for both his family and the world of music. But Clara's inner reserves helped her to survive. She sent their children to boarding schools or to relatives, and within three months she was touring again.

"When I am able to practice regularly, then I really feel totally in my element; it is as though an entirely different mood comes over me, lighter, freer, and everything seems happier and more gratifying ... The practice of art is, after all, a great part of my inner self. To me, it is the very air I breathe."

Clara performed in public for 63 years, from the age of nine to the age of 72. She often said that her stamina and good health were the result of her early training with her father and the long walks that she kept up all her life. Clara's influence on the world of music took many different forms. Through her brilliant interpretations of their work, she helped several important musicians to establish their reputations, including Robert Schumann, Johannes Brahms, and Frédéric Chopin. Pianists customarily appeared onstage with other musical and theatrical performers, but Clara started the trend of appearing alone, as a respected musician capable of sustaining an entire evening's performance. Her many distinguished students went on to work in conservatories all over the world. She edited her husband's musical works, preparing them for publication.

Along with the energy she poured into her career, Clara was also a loving mother and grandmother. Sadly, four of her children died before she did, and one son had to live in a mental hospital. Even though she eventually reconciled with her father, Frederick remained difficult and distant. After he died, Clara wrote in her diary: "Although we had many disagreements it never affected my love for him, a love which all my life long has been heightened by gratitude. How many years he dedicated to me, to the exclusion of all else."

Clara Schumann lived through many tragedies, but her deep, abiding love for music kept her going. When she died at the age of 77, her grandson was in the room with her, playing a piece by Robert Schumann. It was the last music she ever heard.

SPEND MORE TIME WITH CLARA

Clara Schumann, Piano Virtuoso by Susanna Reich
This intriguing book about Clara's life includes pictures of Clara and her family, programs from her concerts, and excerpts from her diaries and letters.

Clara, Robert & Johannes: Theme and Variations by Clara & Robert Schumann and Johannes Brahms by Veronica Jochum (pianist)
Try to find this CD at your local library. It has Clara's original "Romance" (Opus 3), along with variations and other pieces written by Clara, Robert Schumann, and Johannes Brahms. The CD perfectly illustrates how Clara and Robert influenced each other's music.

Clara Schumann: Complete Piano Works by Jozef de Beenhouwer (pianist)
A good recording of Clara's works.

GIRLS DON'T COUNT

Fanny Mendelssohn

1805–1847

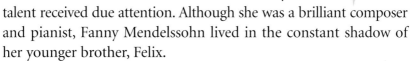

When Queen Victoria invited the composer Felix Mendelssohn to play some of his compositions at her court, she was very impressed by one song in particular: "Italian." She told Felix how much she liked it, and he admitted, "Well, Your Majesty, my sister Fanny wrote that one." This brief moment of recognition was one of the few times in her life that Fanny's talent received due attention. Although she was a brilliant composer and pianist, Fanny Mendelssohn lived in the constant shadow of her younger brother, Felix.

Just 14 years older than Clara Schumann, Fanny, who was equally talented, had to hide her love of music. As a girl born into a wealthy family in Berlin, Germany, she was not expected to earn her living. Performing in public was considered vulgar for someone of her class. Her father found the idea of it shameful, and he forbade Fanny to pursue her music except as a genteel hobby.

Fanny did not have the temperament of a rebel. She adored her brother Felix, and she rejoiced in his success almost as if it were her own. But in another time or another family, the story of the brother-and-sister musical prodigies could have been very different.

Even though Fanny was four years older, she and Felix were so in tune with each other that they might have been twins. Their musical talent was spotted early by their mother, Lea Mendelssohn,

who was an accomplished pianist herself. Abraham, their father, also appreciated music, along with all the other fine things in life. Born into a poor family, he had worked his way up in the banking business, and he was eager to give his children everything money could buy. At the same time, he was a strict

Fanny and Felix Mendelssohn spent many happy hours
together at the piano, sharing their deep love of music.

disciplinarian. He had found success by working hard and sticking
to the rules, and he expected the same of his children.

Fanny and Felix began their day early each morning. Every
minute of their schedule was accounted for: schoolwork with private
tutors, music with the best teachers, fresh air, and exercise. They
didn't have many friends, so they relied on each other for everything. Even when their sister Rebecka and brother Paul were born
(Rebecka became a fine singer and Paul a superb cellist), the two
older children preferred to spend all their time together.

Fanny and Felix spent hours playing the piano and composing,
with Fanny starting a piece and Felix finishing it,
or the other way around. With the encouragement
of their parents and teachers, they freely explored

the intricacies of composition. They were truly happy only when making music in each other's company.

When Fanny was 12, the family moved to a huge house set in seven acres of gardens and woods. A large conservatory, called the Garden Room, was the perfect place to stage performances. Abraham began a custom of holding Sunday musicales, parties where various musicians entertained a large group of fashionable guests. Sooner or later all the famous, wealthy, and aristocratic people in Germany showed up. Fanny started performing at these events when she was 13 or 14, playing the piano. Felix joined in a few years later, standing on a box to conduct a small orchestra.

Fanny planned an ambitious birthday present for her father when she was 13. She memorized all 24 of the preludes and fugues in Bach's *The Well-Tempered Clavier* to play for Abraham at one sitting. To commit this amount of music to memory would be a challenging task for any musician; for a girl of Fanny's age, it was a phenomenal accomplishment. It took her two hours to present her concert. Her father was so dumbfounded that he couldn't find a word to say. Later he worried that the effort had been too much for her.

Abraham was wrong—Fanny loved to work hard at music. She and Felix had a friendly sense of competition that drove them on to greater achievements. But it was clear to Fanny by now that the talent Felix displayed was valued far more than her own. When

In Her Own Words

It must be a sign of talent that I do not give up, though I can get nobody to take an interest in my efforts.

her brother turned 12, his teacher took him to another German city, Weimar, to stay with the famous author Johann Wolfgang von Goethe. Goethe was charmed and impressed by Felix. Fanny stayed at home, living for the letters Felix sent her.

Felix went on to make his mark as one of the major musicians of the 19th century. Fanny cheered him on every step of the way, while reconciling herself to the life of a housewife and mother. She married an artist, Wilhelm Hensel, when she was 24. They moved into a little garden house on the grounds of her parents' estate and soon Fanny gave birth to a son.

With Wilhelm's encouragement, Fanny worked hard on her composing and piano playing, and she started up the Sunday musicales again. They became just as grand as they had been when she was a child, with the addition of a small choir she conducted herself. Fanny made friends with Robert and Clara Schumann, who were great admirers of her music.

Because first her father and then Felix discouraged her, Fanny held back from publishing any of her music until she was 41. It was an instant success, and people wanted more. Sadly, this recognition came too late. One day while she was rehearsing for a Sunday musicale, Fanny had a stroke. She died that same night. Her husband was devastated and Felix himself fell down with a stroke when he heard the news. He recovered enough to publish some more of her music, as a memorial to her, but he died just six months after his beloved sister.

To this day, Fanny Mendelssohn has not received the attention she deserves, and very little of her music has been published. The soaring talent she displayed as a child matured as she developed into an experimental, exciting composer who wrote more than 300 songs, as well as cantatas, sonatas, fugues, and an oratorio. Despite the limits set upon her by her upbringing, she found a way to express herself with joy.

SPEND MORE TIME WITH FANNY

To hear the song that so impressed Queen Victoria, "Italian," go to this website:
http://www2.wwnorton.com/college/music/enj9/shared/jukebox/Hensel_Italien.swf.

Hidden Music: The Life of Fanny Mendelssohn by Gloria Kamen
Get this book if you want to read a really good account of Fanny's life.

THE KID WHO BOUNCED

Buster Keaton

1895–1966

Buster bounced a basketball against the rough stage floor. One, two, three ... Downstage, his father was addressing the packed matinee audience.

"There's only one way to bring up a child," Joe Keaton said confidentially. "Make him mind. Be firm but gentle, that's my motto."

Bounce, bounce, bounce. Buster turned and threw the ball directly at the back of his father's head.

"Never let 'im walk all over you—" said Joe, and the ball knocked him over, splat. Buster leapt after the ball, trampling his father to reach it.

"—like that!" continued Joe, jumping to his feet, grabbing Buster by the back of his jacket, and hurling him across the width of the stage and into the wings. There was a hushed silence. The audience couldn't believe what they'd just seen. A trick gone horribly wrong? Murder, maybe?

Backstage, Buster rolled easily out of the fall, grinning. The stagehand lifted him up and they counted together: "One, two, three, four, five."

Still carrying Buster, the stagehand ambled onstage and handed him to Joe. "Is this yours, Mr. Keaton?" he asked.

Joe took Buster and set him on his feet. "Yup. He's mine."

The audience erupted into laughter. Something deep inside Buster was yelling with glee. He was finally doing the act for a real audience. He'd waited so long for this, watching his parents onstage and standing like a dummy at the side. But today, finally, the manager, Bill Dockstader, had given him his chance. "You're on, kid," he had said in the dressing room after Buster accidentally knocked the pipe out of Dockstader's mouth with his basketball. "Let's see what you can do. Those Gerries

won't bother you here." The "Gerries" were the people who didn't want kids to work onstage, and they had inspectors popping up all over the place.

Back onstage, Buster started chasing an imaginary fly. The fly led him a merry chase, up over a table and then under it. He grabbed a broom and started swatting. The audience kept laughing at him, drowning out the song Joe was singing.

Wham! *The invisible fly landed on the back of Joe's neck, and Buster walloped him with the broom, sending his father sprawling into the footlights. Joe scrambled to his feet, grabbed Buster by his jacket again, and threw him high into the backdrop. By now the audience knew that it was all a gag and the kid wasn't getting hurt. As Buster slid to the floor, they roared.*

Next Buster's mother appeared in a fancy gown, sashaying across the stage. Joe aimed a high kick at her hat and off it tumbled. Buster pulled a string at the back of her dress, causing her costume to drop to the floor. Underneath, she was dressed as a clown, just like her son and husband: red wig, baggy pants, and vest.

The Three Keatons bowed to the cheering crowd, and the curtain rang down on Buster's first stage performance.

THE LIVING MOP

Buster Keaton first crawled onstage when he was nine months old. He had escaped from the theatrical trunk that was his playpen backstage and made his way out to where his father was entertaining. Buster peeked out from between Joe's legs at the audience, who laughed heartily at the sudden appearance of a baby with bright button eyes.

The kid was hooked. From then on he took every opportunity to join his parents onstage, clinging to his mother's skirt or his father's trousers. Sometimes his parents tied him to a pole backstage with a long rope, to keep him out of the limelight. As any self-

Joe, Myra, and little Buster made up the Three Keatons, one of the most popular vaudeville acts in the early 1900s.

respecting toddler would, Buster kicked up a fuss and made himself heard. Joe started looking for a way to let his son join the act.

When Buster was five, his father dressed him up in a clown outfit identical to his own. He sat Buster down at the edge of the stage and instructed him to watch. That didn't last long. Soon Buster was bopping around the stage, imitating his father's waddling walk, with his chest stuck out. The boy was a born mimic.

Kids weren't allowed to work onstage in the state of New York, but one afternoon when the Keatons were appearing at the

Wonderland Theater in Wilmington, Delaware, Bill Dockstader, the manager, agreed to let Buster perform at the matinee, since there would be a lot of kids in the audience. Buster brought the house down, and Dockstader immediately offered him a salary of $10 per week.

Offstage, Buster and his dad had been developing an act based on roughhousing for years. Joe Keaton spent some time with his son every night before bedtime. Buster's mother, Myra, called it "Buster's Story Hour." But they weren't reading stories. Instead, Joe would toss the toddler high into the air, up onto the bedroom dresser, or against the wall. Buster had a natural talent for acrobatics, and he quickly learned how to fall without hurting himself. He loved flying through the air and somersaulting out of the falls. Their routine easily translated into a stage act. Buster became known as the "living mop." Myra sewed a suitcase handle on the back of Buster's jacket to make it easier for Joe to pick him up and throw him.

FREEZE THE PUSS

At first, Buster would get up from his falls with a cheeky grin. He was having a ball. But Joe quickly realized that Buster got more laughs from the audience if he kept his face expressionless. He began training his son to keep his face frozen. Even if Buster fell extra hard or Joe clipped him too sharply, he couldn't let any feelings show: no surprise, no pain. If his face twitched, his father would hiss at him, "Face!" or "Freeze the puss!" and the next blow would be even harder. Buster learned to keep his features still, no matter what happened.

Joe was right. The audience loved the fact that Buster never reacted. His sad, frozen clown face became his trademark when he grew up. But he had achieved it through iron discipline when he was still very young.

Child Abuse or Acrobatics?

From our viewpoint, looking back a hundred years, we see a small boy being thrown against walls night after night. Taught to suppress all reactions, he is subject to a series of blows from his father. Off-stage, Buster was sometimes beaten for bad behavior. But it was a different world back then. Children had few rights, and parents had unlimited license to discipline them. Slaps, spankings, and even beatings were considered a normal part of childhood.

Although Myra and Joe were careless parents, there is no doubt of the great affection between Buster and his father. As a grown man, Buster would never have a word spoken against his dad, and he repeatedly hired Joe to act in his movies.

KICKAPOO MAGIC SNAKE OIL

Buster Keaton had been born into a show business family. Joe and Myra Keaton met when they were both performers in traveling medicine shows, a popular form of entertainment in the 1890s. Hundreds of these tent shows crisscrossed the United States, bringing a strange mixture of live music, melodramas (plays with lots of emotion and clearly defined heroes and villains), and comedy acts to remote corners of the country. A so-called "doctor" would open the show by raving about the benefits of a patent medicine, called "snake oil," that promised to cure everything from a bad cold to a broken leg. Many of the medicines did contain some snake oil, a substance that is supposed to kill pain, but the main ingredient was alcohol. The bottles of medicine sold well and helped warm up the audience for the acts that followed.

Myra could play the cornet (a type of trumpet), the bass, the fiddle, the piano, and the saxophone. She was tiny, but she had a lively stage presence. Joe was an expert at the art of legomania, which included spectacular high kicks and comic dancing. Joe and Myra went from one job to the next. When they worked for

Dr. Hill's Medicine Show, they made friends with two fellow performers, Harry Houdini and his wife, Bess. While Dr. Hill made extravagant claims about Kickapoo Magic Snake Oil, Joe and Harry Houdini went up and down the aisles selling bottles to the crowd. Later, Houdini performed his specialty: escaping from locked handcuffs. He would eventually go on to make his mark as a world-famous magician and escape artist.

BORN A BUSTER

Buster was born in a boardinghouse during a stopover in a Kansas railway town called Picqua. He slept in a suitcase for the first few months of his life. The Keatons toured the mining camps of Kansas, often living in tents and sometimes so short of money that Joe would buy a train ticket for Myra and the baby while he walked to the next town.

Buster was named Joseph Frank Keaton, after his father and his grandfather. How he got nicknamed Buster is shrouded in showbiz legend. According to one version of the story, when he was six months old he somehow tumbled down a long flight of stairs. Harry Houdini picked him up and the baby started to laugh. Houdini said admiringly, "That's some buster [meaning a bad fall] your baby took." A "buster" also referred to someone who was tough and full of beans—and the smallest Keaton was all of that. Whatever its origins, the name stuck.

THE KID WHO COULDN'T BE DAMAGED

Tornadoes! Fires! Train wrecks! Falling bricks! Wringer washers! The young Buster Keaton had lived through them all.

That's how the stories went, anyway. It's hard to separate truth from fiction. Joe Keaton loved to tell tall tales, and Buster later retold the stories about his many escapes from death until they gained a life of their own. Throughout his vaudeville career Joe toted around a huge old typewriter on which he composed articles for the entertainment newspapers. It was all a form of advertising for the act, and

A Wooden Friend

When Buster was seven, the Three Keatons appeared in a show with the great ventriloquist Trovollo. Ventriloquists master the art of talking without moving their lips, throwing their voice so it sounds as if it's coming from somewhere else. Traditionally, they have one wooden dummy or doll who sits on their lap and talks back to them. Trovollo had 10.

Trovollo held conversations with his dummies offstage as well as in his act, asking them how they had slept or what they thought about the weather. Buster was never quite sure if the dummies were really talking or not. He particularly liked a red-haired doll, and one day Trovollo made the dummy say he would like to be Buster's friend. Buster didn't have any children as friends; he spent all his time around adults. So he made up his mind to kidnap the dummy.

One night while the grown-ups were playing cards, Buster sneaked out of the boardinghouse and went back to the empty theater. Trovollo saw him go and managed to get there ahead of him.

The dark theater was full of shadows and whispers. Trovollo's wooden dummies were lying under a sheet backstage. When Buster raised the edge of the sheet, the red-haired dummy sat up and said sharply to him, "Don't touch me, boy, or I'll tell your old man!"

Terrified, Buster turned and fled, running all the way back to the boardinghouse. In the kitchen, his parents were sitting with Trovollo, laughing at the trick he had played. Buster went upstairs and threw himself sobbing onto his bed. His mother came up to comfort him.

"It's only a wooden doll, Buster," she said, patting him on the back. But he kept crying. It wasn't just because he had been so frightened and the grown-ups had laughed at him. Buster was also crying because he'd lost the chance to make a friend.

Joe relied on exaggeration and his fertile imagination to feed the image of Buster as "The Kid Who Couldn't Be Damaged."

When Buster was two, he got his finger stuck in a wringer washer. They had to take the washing machine apart screw by screw, and Buster's finger was so badly mangled that the doctor had to amputate it at the first knuckle. This actually happened. But according to Joe, later that same day Buster threw a brick up in the air and it cut his forehead when it came down. Then, as Buster was sitting in a second-floor window recovering from the excitement, a tornado snatched him up, whirled him high into the sky, and deposited him unhurt a few blocks away. This led to Joe calling Buster "The Kid Who Rode a Cyclone."

As a troupe of traveling performers, the Keatons had their share of mishaps. There were a couple of fires in boardinghouses where they were staying, and a fire in a theater in Chicago while they were onstage. And yes, there were train crashes. Joe made the most of every disaster with an Irish storyteller's zeal for drama.

Coney Island Amusement Park had something for everyone: Ferris wheels, merry-go-rounds, swimming, high-diving exhibitions, bicycle races, boxers, clowns, acrobats, and vaudeville entertainers.

BRIGHT LIGHTS OF VAUDEVILLE

From about 1890 until 1930, vaudeville reigned supreme in North America and England as the most popular form of entertainment. Before radio and movies became widespread, people flocked to vaudeville shows. For a low ticket price they could see 10 to 12 different acts featuring popular singers, musicians, acrobats, and clowns. Cornball humor and sight gags held sway in huge theaters in New York, and traveling troupes took their acts to small towns everywhere.

Myra and Joe got a toehold in the world of vaudeville through their traveling act, with Joe dancing and doing acrobatics and Myra playing her instruments. When Buster joined them, they hit pay dirt. Almost overnight the Three Keatons became one of the most successful vaudeville acts in the country. Their routines were original, unpredictable, and wildly funny. The sight of the tiny boy flying around the stage and driving his father crazy with his tricks was irresistible to audiences of the time. Everyone admired the

The Three Keatons

feisty kid, and the ensuing mayhem had them rolling in the aisles.

When Buster was six, the Three Keatons played Coney Island, a famous amusement park. Buster would eat ice cream and cotton candy all day and go on endless free rides, then appear onstage to deafening applause every night. In some ways it was a dream life for a kid, but Buster had to work hard and develop the discipline of an adult. His part in the act depended on quick thinking and split-second timing. Joe and Buster delivered stunning blows to each other onstage. They were both expert tumblers and acrobats, but a small mistake could result in an injury. Joe was renowned for his high kicks, and once he hit Buster in the head in the wrong spot. Buster was unconscious for 18 hours. When he came to, the doctor advised him to rest for a few days, but two hours later Buster was flying through the air. He couldn't bear to miss a show.

It was a matter of pride for Buster not to wear any protective padding. Joe sometimes wore padding in his trousers or a steel cap under his wig to protect his head. Occasionally he forgot to wear the padding, but Buster's punches came just as hard. Joe would reel with the impact.

The Three Keatons were unique in show business. No other acts imitated them. When children appeared onstage, they were usually darling little cutie-pies with lacy costumes and golden ringlets, not hell-raisers in red fright wigs bent on destruction. Today the act would not be tolerated. Violence to children is no longer considered amusing. But at the time, the contrast between the rules and propriety of Victorian society and the anarchy of the feuding Keatons proved to be mesmerizing. There was only one hitch: every time Buster appeared onstage, he was breaking the law.

Vaudeville Lives On

The decade from 1900 to 1910 represented the golden days of vaudeville. Stages across the United States and Canada shimmered with the talent of ragtime piano players, opera singers, barbershop quartets, tap dancers, jugglers, and magicians. Everything was jumbled together in a slap-happy mix that guaranteed one thing for the audience: rollicking entertainment.

In the 1920s and 1930s, radio and movies largely replaced the live variety show, and vaudeville became a thing of the past. But its influence spread through the performing arts as vaudeville performers such as the Three Stooges and the Marx Brothers moved into film, bringing their comic routines with them. When television became popular in the 1950s and 1960s, many vaudeville-style skits were revived and used in shows such as *I Love Lucy* and *The Dick Van Dyke Show* (both of which can be seen today in reruns). *The Ed Sullivan Show*, popular on TV from the late 1940s until the early 1970s, used the same format as vaudeville, featuring musicians, comics, and even circus acts. More recently, Steve Martin's pratfalls and Rowan Atkinson's bumbling Mr. Bean both owe a debt to vaudeville's slapstick routines.

OUTSMARTING THE CHILD POLICE

For centuries children have worked alongside their parents—on farms, in shops, and in factories. But by the end of the 19th century, people were starting to believe that this was wrong. In Buster's time, kids still peddled newspapers on the streets, played fiddles on ferryboats, shined shoes, and worked in sweatshops making clothes. And some kids worked in the theater.

In 1875 a public-spirited citizen named Elbridge T. Gerry founded a society to protect children. The organization helped pass laws that forbade children under the age of 16 from working. Inspectors were sent out to find working children and bring their parents to court. The laws governing child labor in New York State were strict: No one under the age of seven was allowed to set foot onstage. Children under 16 could not perform acrobatics, juggle, sing, dance, or do high-wire work.

From the beginning of Buster's career, Joe wiggled and wangled to get his son onstage. He started out by saying that Buster was seven, not five, and applied for a permit for him to appear as a "comedian"—one type of performance that was not covered by the law. To hedge his bets, Joe started a rumor that Buster was not a child at all, but a midget. He and Myra dressed their son up in a three-piece suit, hat, and briefcase and had promotional pictures taken of him. He traveled with his own set of luggage, the trunks and suitcases all marked "BUSTER."

The Gerry Society was formed to protect children like these seven-year-old twins, who started selling newspapers on the street in 1908, when they were six.

Buster came to dread the Gerry inspectors. They would appear on a Monday and subject him to intense questioning about his age and his act. If they were satisfied, they would let him appear that night. Joe would tame down the first show so as not to shock them with the image of Buster slamming into sets and sliding headfirst across the splintery wooden stage. By Tuesday, though, the act would be a little wilder, and it would slowly work itself back to its usual madness by Friday.

WHO NEEDS SCHOOL?

When he was grown up, Buster loved to embellish the incidents from his childhood to make a good story even better. He told the tale of how he went to school for only one morning. Supposedly, he disrupted the class with standard one-liners from vaudeville acts and the principal asked him not to return. According to Buster, these were two of the jokes that had his classmates rolling on the floor with laughter and the teacher at her wit's end:

Teacher: What's an island?
Buster: A wart on the ocean.
Teacher: Give me a sentence with the word delight *in it.*
Buster: The vind blew in the vindow and blew out de light.

His parents gave up on the idea of school for Buster. Daily classes didn't make sense for a child who was up late every night and had performances most afternoons. Besides, the family never stayed in one place for more than a few weeks at a time.

Joe Keaton assured the concerned public that his son had private tutors on the road, but there wasn't much evidence of this. Mostly Buster picked up reading, writing, and doing sums on his own, with some help from his mother. Vaudeville was his real school: everything he needed to learn to become a world-class clown was laid out before his eyes onstage.

LOST: ONE BROTHER AND SISTER

Harry Keaton, better known as Jingles, was born when Buster was nine. A couple of years later, Buster's sister Louise came along. Buster was pressed into duty as a babysitter in addition to his responsibilities for the family business. By the age of 12 he was performing one or two shows daily and arranging hotel bookings and train reservations. One day he managed to lose Jingles and Louise in Boston Common, a big park in the middle of town. Luckily, the police found them.

Buster wasn't too keen on sharing the limelight with his little brother and sister. His mother and father came to agree with him. Neither Louise nor Jingles had Buster's love of performing, his reckless physical courage, or his talent as a comedian. They were both packed off to boarding schools.

Buster and his brother Jingles in the Browniekar he bought when he was 13. The popular toy car could go 10 miles (16 km) an hour.

BATHING-SUIT SUMMERS

For entertainers who are nearly always on tour, home is whatever town they find themselves in. For the Keatons, it was most convenient to live in boardinghouses. But when Buster was 14, his parents bought a little cottage on Lake Muskegon in Michigan. About 200 theater people retreated to the picturesque lake each summer.

The three smaller Keatons ran wild at the lake—swimming, boating, and making friends with kids their own age. Buster showed an aptitude for baseball; with his natural athleticism and sharp sense of timing, he could have pursued a professional career in the sport. Always the clown, he enjoyed surprising his opponents on the field by doing backflips, cartwheels, or aerobatic dives in the middle of a play.

Lake Muskegon also offered Buster the chance to play jokes on unsuspecting visitors. When he saw strangers sitting on the deck at the sailing club, Buster would ride his bike down the hill at top speed and shoot off the edge of the dock, bike and all. Another favorite prank was to hurl first his brother, then his sister, then himself off the porch of their cottage and over a cliff. People passing in boats would shriek, thinking the children had fallen to their deaths. Actually, they'd tumbled unhurt onto a soft hill of sand.

BANISHED FROM BROADWAY

The Gerry Society kept hounding the Keatons, and a couple of times Joe was charged with child brutality. In response, he brought Buster before two different New York City mayors and had his son take off his clothes so they could look for bruises. Buster didn't have any; he knew how to fall.

The child police finally caught up with Joe when Buster was officially 14 (he was really only 12). The whole family were appearing at a charity concert. The management had assured Joe they had permits for the children to be onstage. But they didn't, and the Gerries were on the case in no time. Joe was arrested and fined, and the family was banned from performing in New York State for two years. This was a terrible blow for them all. Banishment meant hitting the road, where the work was harder and the money not so good. Somehow they managed, and two years later they returned to New York with a big ad in the trade papers: "BUSTER IS 16!!!" (Of course, he was really only 14!)

In His Own Words

"Because I was also a born hambone, I ignored any bumps or bruises I may have got at first on hearing audiences gasp, laugh, and applaud ... I was not brought up thinking life would be easy. I always expected to work hard for my money and to get nothing I did not earn."

THE THREE KEATONS BREAK UP

As a troublemaking little kid, Buster was the star of the Three Keatons. As he grew up, the act changed. When Buster got too big for his father to throw across the stage, the two of them worked out a slapstick clown routine. The act was different each time, and people started coming daily just to see what would happen next. Their antics kept the audience in stitches.

As Joe grew older, the grueling physical demands of the act took their toll on him. He had always been a bit of a drinker, but now his alcohol intake increased to the danger point. Buster tried to cover for him, both onstage and with theater management. But Joe tended to be violent when he was drunk, and their act became more perilous. Joe had ongoing feuds with more than one theater owner. Once he ran offstage after a producer and chased him through the streets of New York, right in the middle of a show. Buster recited verses and joked around until his father reappeared.

Because Joe was so hard to get along with, the Keatons lost their place in the big vaudeville theaters and were forced to tour all the time. Finally one day, in the middle of a tour, Buster and his mother took a train out of town without even leaving Joe a note. The Three Keatons were finished.

WHAT HAPPENED NEXT

Joe caught up with Myra and Buster at Lake Muskegon. The three of them made up, but it was clear the family would never be going on the road again. Buster moved to New York to pursue his career. He got a part in a Broadway musical, but soon gave it up to devote himself to films. He teamed up with another comical star, Fatty Arbuckle, and learned how to translate his stage know-how to the silver screen.

Between 1920 and 1929, Buster's output was amazing. He wrote, directed, starred in, and produced 12 feature films and 19 shorter ones. Critics and audiences agree that his film *The General* is one of the best movies ever made. He brought his daring physical comedy to the screen along with his split-second timing and sad, still clown's face.

When the talkies replaced silent films in the 1930s, Buster lost artistic control of his films. But he kept working in movies and later

In Buster's movies he tried hard to get the pretty girl, but he often ended up behind bars. This scene is from *Cops* (1922).

television. In the 1960s there was a revival of interest in his silent movies, and he is recognized today as a comic genius.

Buster Keaton married three times and had two sons. His third marriage, to Eleanor Norris, was the happiest, and he stayed with Eleanor until his death in 1966 at the age of 70. The bouncing boy who was so desperate to get onstage at the age of five rose to the top of his profession twice: once as a child star on the vaudeville stage and once as the creator and star of silent films. His work has inspired directors, actors, and clowns for more than eight decades.

Daredevils and Clowns

What do Jackie Chan, Johnny Depp, and Mr. Noodle from *Sesame Street* all have in common? They are just three of the many performers whose work has been influenced by Buster Keaton.

Jackie Chan is famous for his kung fu movies. His most successful films blend comedy and action, and he says that Buster Keaton is a continuing source of inspiration for him. Like Buster, Jackie prides himself on doing his own stunts, and he often risks his life in the process. The Hong Kong actor has re-created many of Buster's classic on-screen stunts. In *Project A-2* a wall teeters over and crashes, with Jackie remaining unhurt as it falls all around him. Buster did a similar scene with a falling house in *Steamboat Bill Jr.* If the house had fallen even slightly off the mark, it would have killed him.

When Johnny Depp played Sam, an eccentric character in the film *Benny and Joon*, he based much of his performance on Buster's classic clown. In one shot in the movie he is even shown reading a book about Buster Keaton.

Mr. Noodle appears in "Elmo's World" on *Sesame Street*. He performs various activities without speaking, just as if he were in a silent movie. Bill Irwin, the actor who plays Mr. Noodle, makes people laugh with the same type of slapstick humor Buster Keaton so brilliantly employed.

SPEND MORE TIME WITH BUSTER

Get some Buster Keaton DVDs from your local video store or library. They are all very funny, but these are my favorites:

The General, 1927
Most of the action takes place on a train named The General during the American Civil War. Buster plays a brave engineer up against a group of enemy spies.

Convict 13, 1920
Watch for the scene in the prison yard where Buster starts spinning a basketball on a rope, in a re-creation of one of his standard vaudeville acts with the Three Keatons.

Sherlock Jr., 1924
In this fanciful classic, Buster walks right inside the movie screen in a cinema and joins the cast of characters in a wild dream that has him stepping from a mountaintop to a lion's den to a desert.

http://www.busterkeaton.com
This website created by the International Buster Keaton Society has lots of fun stuff about Buster, including a calendar of when his films are showing on television. It also provides a summary of the plot of every one of his movies.

A BOY, A BOOK, AND A PACK OF CARDS

Dai Vernon

1894–1992

When David Verner first started learning card tricks, his hands were so small that he had to use a miniature deck. He thought nothing of practicing tricks for 10 hours a day. The love of magic took hold of David at a very young age, and it never let him go.

David's parents, James and Helen Verner, were a respectable middle-class couple living in Ottawa, Canada, at the end of the Victorian era. Performers of any kind were considered immoral by the Verners and their friends. After David gave a stunning display of his talent in a school variety show, Mrs. Verner was reduced to tears. "People will think I adopted you from a circus!" she wailed.

Undaunted, David spent every waking moment pursuing new tricks. He began with the family encyclopedia, which gave a few examples of "legerdemain" (sleight of hand). He sent away for books from magic supply houses. He sought out other boys who did magic and picked up what he could from them.

Sleight of hand is a technique that relies on manual dexterity, misdirection, and psychology to deceive the audience. The magician has to practice the physical moves for months, even years, to be able to do them so smoothly and quickly that they are almost invisible. He must also learn how to control his audience, making them look where he wants them to look (misdirection), and this is where psychology comes into play. David became a master of sleight of hand as a boy, manipulating both the cards and his audience with the style and confidence of an adult. He loved to play tricks on his

friends on the way home from school, sometimes planting marked cards ahead of time in strategic locations.

Luckily for David, Ottawa was on the vaudeville circuit. He went to see every magician who came to town. He would wangle his way backstage to talk to the masters and see what he could learn from them. When he was only seven, he managed to fool one of these visiting magicians, Howard Thurston, with a card trick.

At the age of 10, David came across a book that would change his life: *The Expert at the Card Table: A Treatise on the Science and Art of Manipulating Cards* by S.W. Erdnase. He memorized it word for word and eventually mastered every card trick in it. The book itself was surrounded by mystery: no one was sure who had written it. S.W. Erdnase was a pseudonym for someone—but who?

Dai Vernon got a big kick out of hoodwinking his audience with stunning, up-close card tricks that defied explanation.

A cardsharp certainly, a gambler most likely—or maybe a great magician? What made this book so remarkable was its elegant, detailed description of all the important techniques for cheating at cards, techniques that were regularly used by magicians as well as cardsharps. The simple illustrations and meticulous text provided step-by-step instructions for deception. Many years later people came to believe that the book had been written by a notorious criminal named E.S. Andrews (S.W. Erdnase spelled backwards).

David practiced his magic tricks everywhere. He even did them at church, hiding his hands under his father's hat, but the minister spotted him and he got in big trouble. At school he liked geography best because he could hide his tricks behind the big atlas. Whenever he was caught, his teacher confiscated his cards or magic props for the rest of the term.

David had a real talent for drawing, too. His parents wanted him to use his artistic ability to enter engineering, but he had other ideas. He was assigned to a desk job during the First World War, and when it ended he went to New York to pursue a career as "Dai Vernon, Magician." Dai was his boyhood nickname, and he used Vernon because it was easier to pronounce.

"I was born to deceive."

Earlier magicians had emphasized flamboyant presentation and grand illusions; Dai specialized in a natural-looking, close-up style of magic. His elegant performances appealed to a cultivated, well-heeled audience, and for a while he spent much of his time confounding rich and famous guests at small society parties and on board luxury cruise ships.

One of Dai's earliest triumphs was to hoodwink Harry Houdini, one of the most famous illusionists in the world (see also page 66). Houdini boasted that he could figure out any card trick if he saw it performed three times. Dai took up the challenge, proceeding to do one of his best tricks. He asked Houdini to pick a card then write his initials on it. Dai put it in second place in the deck. Then he turned over the top card and—presto!—somehow the card with Houdini's initials on it had jumped from second to first place. He did the trick seven times, but Houdini couldn't figure it out. From then on Dai billed himself as "The Man Who Fooled Houdini."

Some people consider Dai Vernon the most influential magician of the 20th century. He had the unique ability to transform a classic magic trick by reducing it to a series of fluid, streamlined moves. Dai lectured and performed in England and throughout North America, and other magicians flocked to study with him. He became known as "the Professor." In the 1960s Dai moved to California, where he settled into the Magic Castle, a club for magicians in Hollywood. There he reigned until his death in the 1990s at age 98. All the great magicians had come to learn from him, including John Carney, Persi Diaconis, Doug Henning, and Ricky Jay.

From the age of six, Dai Vernon used his skills to flummox and delight his audiences. Truly a "wonder kid," he made magic tricks even more magical with his brilliant innovations.

SPEND MORE TIME WITH DAI

Dai Vernon: the Spirit of Magic
This is a very good television program about Dai. It is part of a series called *The Canadians: Biographies of a Nation*, which might be available at your library or video store. In it you can see footage of him doing his cups-and-balls routine, and several of his card tricks are demonstrated.

The Expert at the Card Table by S.W. Erdnase
This classic is still in print, and magicians and cardsharps agree that it remains one of the very best books about card tricks. If you try to learn just one of the techniques, you will get an idea of how much time young David Verner put in to master these tricks.

HARMONICA HOTSHOT

Stevie Wonder

1950–

"**W**ill you just quit jumping around, Stevie?" said Martha Reeves. "You're gonna rip my dress."

"Sorry, Martha, sorry, Martha," chanted Stevie, still jumping. He bumped into her again.

"Stevie!" she hollered. "Just stand still a minute!"

But Stevie couldn't stand still. There wasn't much room backstage, with Martha and her group, the Vandellas, and their musicians all squeezed into the wings, plus the stagehands and two—or was it three?—of the singers in the Miracles milling around. The show was about to start, and Stevie was so worked up he just had to jump.

Bill Murray, the master of ceremonies for the Motortown Revue, spoke into Stevie's ear. "Keep your shirt on, Stevie. Just a few more minutes."

"How big's the audience, Bill?" asked Stevie. Although he couldn't see, he recognized people by their voices. Once he'd met someone a couple of times, he could always identify them.

"Standing room only, Stevie. They're rarin' to go. Listen."

Bill twitched aside the edge of the heavy curtain. Stevie could smell the faint cloud of dust that rose as the curtain moved. Beyond the stage, the theater was full of a rustling, chattering, restless crowd, finding their seats, calling out to each other, laughing.

"Mmmmm," murmured Stevie. He could feel his excitement growing. It had been playing bongos on the inside of his stomach for the last hour in anticipation of the evening's show.

The stage manager sidled up to Bill. "Time, Bill. Go for it."

A rush of energy made Stevie jump again, bumping into Martha.

"Stevie, I swear!" she hissed at him through clenched teeth. "Just you wait till after the show and I'll tell you exactly what I think of you! And if you don't get off the stage tonight when your song's over, so help me, I'll make you wish you never were born!"

Stevie laughed and pinched Martha's bottom. "You don't mean that, honey," he said.

"Why, you little ..." Martha sputtered. But the lights were coming up and the curtains were pulling back and Bill was bouncing onto the stage. Martha smiled as she put her arm around her friend's shoulder and gave him a quick hug. "Knock 'em dead, Stevie," she whispered.

"Don't mind if I do," said Stevie to himself. This was it, then. He wiped his sweaty hands on his pants and gripped his harmonica tightly. Bill was giving his usual intro.

"Let me introduce to you a young man who is only 12 years old ... and he is already considered a genius of our time. Ladies and gentlemen, let's make him feel happy with a nice ovation as we meet and greet—Little Stevie Wonder!"

A roar went up from the audience as Stevie walked onstage. He knew exactly how many steps to take till he was in front of the mike. The crowd cheered and clapped.

The drums started a roll. "Yeah!" Stevie called out to the slowly quickening beat of the drum. "Yeah! Now, I want you to clap your hands," he called to the audience. "Come on. Come on. Yeah! Stomp your feet, jump up and down, do anything that you WANNA do. Yeah! Yeah!"

As the drum kicked in, Stevie started a slow, simple riff on his harmonica. When the rest of the band came in, he kept on playing, getting a bit fancier with each phrase. The audience were still clapping, yelling out now and then. Stevie was carrying them along with him, teasing out each note. He'd performed this tune, "Fingertips," a hundred times, and every time it was just as sweet, just as smooth. Stevie danced around the stage. This was what he lived for—making the music and keeping the audience with him every step of the way. When his number was over, he broke into "Mary Had a Little Lamb" on the harmonica. That always made them laugh.

What came next was the most fun. Stevie started back in on the tune, with the audience encouraging him. He was stomping his feet and singing, "Goodbye, goodbye," pretending to leave but intent on staying. "Let's swing it one more time."

This was what Martha had been talking about. She was on next, and he was stepping all over her time. Stevie knew that Clarence, the songwriter, would soon come out and get him. It was all part of the gag. Stevie laughed as he tore his sunglasses off and hurled them into the crowd. When they cheered, he whipped off his bow tie and threw that out too. He was sweating and laughing as Clarence grabbed him and carried him off the stage. When Clarence put him down, Stevie could hear the audience still screaming for more.

"You little creep!" said Martha. "How 'm I gonna top that?"

Martha Reeves (middle) and her singing group, the Vandellas, in England for a tour in 1964. Martha was like a big sister to Stevie.

POOR, BLACK, AND BLIND

Stevland Judkins came into the world four weeks early, on May 13, 1950. He was so small the doctors popped him into an incubator, where he stayed for a month. Sometime during those four weeks something went terribly wrong. The baby was given too much oxygen, and a thick substance formed over his eyes, making him blind.

As a clumsy but well-meaning teacher later pointed out to him, Stevie was born with three strikes against him. Black people in the United States in the 1950s faced widespread prejudice. For most blacks, life was an uphill struggle to make a living and find a place in the world. Born to a single mother with two older children already, Stevie was dirt poor with few prospects. With the further handicap of blindness, his future didn't look too good.

But Lulu Mae Hardaway, Stevie's mother, had other ideas.

TWELVE MILES FROM THE NORTH POLE

Stevie was born in a small city called Saginaw in northern Michigan, near the U.S.–Canada border. When Stevie was older, his stepfather would tease the kids by saying Saginaw was only twelve miles from the North Pole. For a long time Stevie believed him. The place was bitterly cold in winter, and there wasn't much work available for a black woman with three little kids on her hands. When Stevie was three, his mother moved the family south to the bigger city of Detroit. Detroit is the headquarters for the giant car factories General Motors and Ford. There were a lot of black people living there, many of them in dire poverty. But Lulu Mae found work cleaning houses and managed to support her sons. It was tough; sometimes they were hungry and often they were cold. Stevie and his brothers, Calvin and Milton, occasionally stole coal to burn for warmth.

Stevie and his brothers had two different fathers. After she moved to Detroit, Lulu Mae reunited with Paul Hardaway, the father of her older sons, and had three more children. But all the while she had Stevie's welfare on her mind. It broke her heart to see him stumble as he was learning to walk. She took her little boy to eye specialists and faith healers to see if his sight could be restored, but no one could help him.

Lulu Mae was a devout Baptist. Her minister told her that God would make up for Stevie's blindness by giving him other abilities. She already knew he was a very special child, with a joyous outlook on life and a devilish sense of curiosity. And he had this strange habit of drumming on the furniture.

ALL THE WORLD'S A DRUM

When Stevie was two, he picked up a couple of spoons and beat out a rhythm on the kitchen table. Then he started banging away on a pot. Everything was a drum for this little boy: tin cans filled with marbles, bottles—even walls. The kid was full of rhythm that just had to get out. At Christmas he was given toy drums that he promptly beat to death, destroying them in a matter of days with his enthusiastic playing.

Stevie got to try out some real drums one day when his family went to a picnic where there was a band. The drummer placed the boy on his lap and let him play. The audience tossed him quarters, and Stevie kept them in his pocket, where he loved the jingling sound they made. When one sense is taken away, the others often compensate by becoming stronger. Stevie's hearing was especially acute. He used to play a game with his brothers in which they would drop a coin on the table and he would tell them whether it was a quarter, a dime, or a nickel. Stevie was completely tuned in to the world of sound.

Just as the minister said, God had given Stevie something to make up for his blindness; apparently he had music coursing through his veins. Lulu Mae was somewhat comforted. She had always wanted a musician in the family. Maybe Stevie would be okay after all.

Finally, at a Lions Club Christmas party for blind children, Stevie got his own set of drums. He started playing them upside down. When he was told to turn them over, he objected—he liked the sound he was making on the metal struts. This originality was to become one of Stevie Wonder's trademarks. He was going to take music to a place no one had ever gone before.

BARN-HOPPING

Lulu Mae had a hard time keeping up with her hell-bent-for-leather son. Stevie had curiosity to burn and was always getting into something. She assigned his two older brothers to be his protectors. Although Calvin and Milton took their job seriously, walking Stevie to school and watching out for him at recess, they couldn't resist leading him into trouble at every opportunity. Stevie tagged along on their expeditions, learning to shoot a slingshot (he loved the noise the rocks made bouncing off stuff) and taking tires off abandoned cars and rolling them down the alley. The brothers played on the railroad tracks and did some barn-hopping. A popular pastime for the neighborhood boys, this involved jumping from roof to roof across the sheds and outbuildings in people's backyards. Stevie had a great time throwing himself into the air and somehow landing safely on the other side. He didn't let his lack of sight stop him from anything.

Blind Bluesmen

There have been many gifted blind musicians. Blind Lemon Jefferson (1893–1929) was a legendary blues player with a fast guitar and a high-pitched voice. He had a big influence on the blues players who came after him. Ray Charles (1930–2004) was a wildly popular piano player and singer who brought soul music into the mainstream. Sonny Terry (1911–1986) played blues harmonica and sang with his stage partner, Brownie McGhee.

LEARNING FROM THE RADIO

When Stevie was four, an uncle gave him a toy harmonica from his key chain. It had only four holes (full-sized harmonicas have 10 or more holes), but Stevie taught himself to play it. A few years later he was given a proper harmonica, and after that there was no stopping him.

Every night Stevie listened to a local radio show called *Sundown*, which played popular rhythm and blues songs. He listened carefully for the harmonica parts and then imitated them, practicing constantly until he perfected them. He didn't consider it work. The more he played, the more he discovered: new chords, new melodies, and new styles. He was fascinated with what the harmonica could do, and he gradually built up his own style of playing. Stevie became a virtuoso (a master) of the harmonica before the age of 10.

Stevie loved playing the piano too. He started when he was three, with easy tunes like "Three Blind Mice." As he grew older, he would just hear a song and then play it. He spent so much time pounding out tunes on his neighbor's piano that when she moved away she gave it to him.

MOVING IT TO THE STREET

Music consumed Stevie day and night. He paired up with John Glover, a friend who sang and played the guitar, and they performed on front porches, in back alleys, and on street corners. Stevie played the drums and harmonica, and he and John both delivered their renditions of the popular hits of the time—especially the music of black artists Marvin Gaye and Smokey Robinson. The two kids were a scream, with spot-on imitations of the stars that delighted their audiences. Soon they were playing at parties.

In the early 1960s, popular black music was taking off in Detroit. Gaye and Robinson were riding the crest of a wave, and Motown Records had just been created to showcase the talents of exciting new black musicians. Stevie was in the right place at the

The Happy Harmonica

Harmonicas are cheap and they fit in your pocket. The harmonica made its way to North America from Europe in the 1850s and soon became popular among young and old, rich and poor. Abraham Lincoln was said to carry a harmonica to play when he needed cheering up, and soldiers on both sides in the American Civil War could be heard blowing tunes on their harmonicas in between battles.

The harmonica has many nicknames: mouth organ, harp, hobo harp, French harp, tin sandwich, lickin' stick, blues harp, Mississippi saxophone. Its evocative wailing particularly suits both the blues and folk music, but it is also popular in country music, jazz, pop, and rock and roll. Sometimes the harmonica is even featured in classical music.

Because the harmonica is a reed instrument, the notes are formed when the player blows into the holes and sets the reeds vibrating. Almost anyone can learn to play the harmonica, but few people play it really well. Some of the world's best harmonica players had colorful names: Slim Harpo, Sugar Blue, Peter Madcap Ruth, Greg "Fingers" Taylor, Kirk Jellyroll Johnson, Jean "Toots" Thielemans.

right time, and he had talent to burn. It wasn't long before he drew the attention of Ronnie White, a member of Smokey Robinson's band, the Miracles. Ronnie's brother Gerald knew Stevie, and he'd told Ronnie he had to hear this amazing kid who played and sang like a pro.

LAUNCHED: ONE CAREER

Stevie didn't just play music; he made it up, experimenting with different melodies and lyrics. When he was grown up, he said that he'd composed many, many songs before he was 10, but he never wrote them down. He made up songs for girls he liked, because they got a kick out of it.

Stevie sang his own song "Lonely Boy" for Ronnie White in Ronnie's living room. The singer was so impressed that he arranged for Stevie to see Brian Holland, the talent scout at Motown Records. Stevie auditioned for Brian on the company's front steps, because the studio was booked. Once he'd heard him, Brian knew he had to get this kid in to see the big boss, Berry Gordy.

Gordy was an expert at assessing talent. That was his job: finding the best black musicians and making hit records with them. It wasn't Stevie's voice that particularly impressed him, or the way he played the bongos. When Gordy heard him play the harmonica, he knew this kid would go far. There was something so infectious about the way Stevie blew that harp.
Gordy offered him a contract.

Stevie was only 11. Labor laws required that he keep going to school and that Motown hold his money in trust until he was 21. In the meantime Stevie got a weekly allowance, and his mother was given money to help out with clothes, food, and transportation back and forth to the studio. The little bit of money was a godsend for Lulu Mae.

Motown Magic

Berry Gordy had started his own recording company, Tamla, in 1959. The company name shortly became Motown—after its birthplace, the city of Detroit, affectionately known as Motor City. Motown featured black musicians singing popular rhythm and blues, which was catchy, lively, and easy to dance to. The music quickly rose to the top of the charts, attracting both black and white audiences. Motown acts were famous for their tightly choreographed dance steps and identical costumes. The biggest Motown stars were the Supremes, the Temptations, Marvin Gaye, Smokey Robinson, and, of course, Stevie Wonder.

KID IN A CANDY STORE

The Motown studio was a makeshift affair, affectionately dubbed "the Snakepit" by the artists. Crowded and claustrophobic, the place was chock-full of instruments, speakers, microphones, and a console board for mixing the sound. For Stevie, it was heaven on earth. He spent time there whenever he had a chance, playing the instruments or listening to other artists making records. He often was pressed into service to play or sing backup. The place was a music factory, churning out a single in three or four hours and a full-length album in a week. The office even had a big sign outside that said *Hitsville, U.S.A.*

A red light outside the studio door was illuminated when a song was being recorded. Stevie couldn't see it, and he ruined many a take by barging in. He also managed to stop the show by making funny faces at the singers to break them up. Everyone loved him, although he tried their patience with his mischief.

BOY WONDER

Stevie made friends with everybody at the Motown office. He really hit it off with Martha Reeves, a secretary who was about to become famous with her own singing group, the Vandellas. She treated Stevie like a little brother. He reciprocated by bugging her all day, interrupting her work, and playing tricks on her. Martha taught Stevie all the new dance steps, and they sang duets and told jokes. Like everyone else at Motown, she was astounded by his musical sophistication.

In the studio, Stevie was learning all he could from a legendary Motown drummer, Benny Benjamin. Benny helped Stevie shape his own style of drumming. Another talented Motown regular, Clarence Paul, worked with Stevie on songwriting and singing. People started calling him "the little boy wonder," and this soon translated into "Little Stevie Wonder."

Now he had a stage name as well as a contract. But what next? Berry Gordy wasn't sure what to do with Stevie. There was no doubt the kid was brilliant, but how was he going to fit into the Motown sound? At first Gordy thought they should capitalize on Stevie's blindness, so he had him record a tribute album to Ray Charles. But Stevie's voice wasn't developed enough yet to do justice to Charles's songs. Next they tried a jazz angle. *The Jazz Soul of Little Stevie* had some great recordings of his harmonica playing, but neither it nor the earlier album did very well. Stevie needed a hit single.

The Motown sound that was such a big hit across the U.S.A. all came from this small house in Detroit. The business offices were upstairs and the recording studio was in the basement.

Peace, Love, and Music

In the 1960s, segregation was still enforced in some Southern states, which meant that black and white people were kept separate. When the Motown artists toured the South, they weren't allowed in restaurants and hotels that were designated for "whites only." In some of the theaters where they performed, a rope down the center aisle separated the black side of the audience from the white. Some people even took potshots at the Motown tour bus.

The experience had a profound effect on Stevie. He believed that music should have no color, and he hoped to spread the word through his music that peace and love could conquer hate. In 1966, when he was 16, he recorded a war protest song written by Bob Dylan called "Blowin' in the Wind." It hit the top 10.

As a teenager, Stevie met Martin Luther King, and when the great leader was assassinated in 1968, Stevie wrote some songs to commemorate him. He worked with others in the civil rights movement to get King recognized as an important national figure. Their efforts paid off in 1986 when the third Monday in January was declared Martin Luther King Day.

A WILD RIDE

In 1962, Berry Gordy piled his best acts into a dilapidated bus emblazoned with the words *Motor City Tour*. The bus was overloaded, and so was the schedule. Night after night the Motown musicians played for packed audiences, then spent many hours traveling to the next gig. Often everybody had to sleep on the bus, some of them climbing up onto the luggage racks to stretch out. Stevie didn't make it any easier for people to sleep. He played his harmonica half the night, trying out new songs and bubbling over with energy. The adults had been instructed to keep their language clean around Stevie, but they must have been sorely tested at times.

Stevie loved the overcrowded bus, the cheap hotels, and traveling with some of the best artists in the business. But most of all he loved the shows. Night after night he got to do what he did best—let loose in front of a crowd. Stevie usually opened the show, whipping the audience into a frenzy with his wild harmonica, beseeching them to sing along and clap and stomp their feet. He'd have to be carried offstage, still playing, and this became a standing gag. The musicians who followed his act had to work hard to match the electricity Stevie had generated, but the Motown crew was definitely up to the task. The shows were fantastic, with infectious dance rhythms, strong melodies, and tightly choreographed dancing. The audiences got more than their money's worth, and the tours gave record sales a boost. The schedule played havoc with Stevie's schooling, though, and the Detroit Board of Education decided that he had to stop making music.

GROUNDED

Stevie couldn't believe it. Just when things were really starting to take off for him, it was all coming to a grinding halt. The problem was that some members of Stevie's family and some of his teachers didn't quite believe he was going to make it as a musician. They were concerned that he wasn't spending enough time around kids his own age, and that without an education he wouldn't get very far in life. One teacher informed Stevie that all he could realistically hope for was to make rugs for a living. This comment set Stevie back. He had never thought of his blindness as something to slow him down, but without music his life would fade to black.

As usual, Stevie's mother took a fighting stance. She put an ad in the paper asking for help with keeping Stevie on the road, and soon a nationwide search was on for a tutor. It took a lot of negotiating, but finally the Board of Education relented. If Stevie could spend two weeks out of every four at school and a few hours a day studying while on tour, they would be satisfied. Stevie enrolled at the Michigan School for the Blind, and a tutor, Ted Hull, was hired by Motown.

SCHOOL ON THE ROAD

For the next six years, Ted Hull was Stevie's teacher, road manager, assistant, driver, friend, and substitute father. He had his hands full with the high-spirited boy wonder. But despite his growing fame, Stevie never let audience adulation go to his head. Later Ted would say that the highest compliment he could pay Stevie was that, despite his unusual childhood, Stevie responded to criticism or praise from his teacher just like any other kid.

Ted set out to teach Stevie more than just math and history: he taught him how to survive in a world of sighted people. Ted Hull was himself partly blind, and one of the things he demonstrated to Stevie was how to find his way around a new hotel room. Most hotel rooms are set up in the same way, and Hull showed Stevie where he could usually find the phone, TV, and bathroom. Ted taught Stevie the value of money, too, doling out an allowance every week and helping him identify foreign currency when they traveled in Europe. Ted said later that he was harder on Stevie than he might have been on his own child—but it paid off. A few rules and some discipline helped keep Stevie on a steady keel.

"Many years ago, but not so long ago, there were those who said, 'Well, you have three strikes against you: You're black, you're blind, and you're poor.' But God said to me, 'I will make you rich in the spirit of inspiration, to inspire others as well as create music to encourage the world to a place of oneness and hope and positivity.' I believed Him and not them.

—from an acceptance speech for an honorary Doctor of Music degree at the University of Alabama at Birmingham in 1996

While they were on tour, Ted got up early every morning to prepare for the daily lesson, then taught Stevie between about 10 a.m. and 1 p.m. They were often out at performances until midnight. Sometimes Ted stepped in to stop Stevie from spending too many hours taping or working too many nights in a row. And since Ted was one of the only white people on the tour, it was often up to him to negotiate with bigoted hotel or restaurant owners to get some service for the black musicians.

When he was back in Detroit, Stevie attended school, where he had the opportunity to spend time around other kids who were blind. Stevie threw himself into school activities—singing in the choir, swimming, wrestling, skating, and making lifelong friends.

FAMOUS FINGERTIPS

Berry Gordy decided to tape a show and package it as Stevie's next record. The hit single they'd been waiting for finally arrived in the summer of 1963. "Fingertips" was a song written by Clarence Paul and Henry Cosby, with a rousing gospel opening and runaway harmonica solos. It always brought the house down in live performance, and the single captured Stevie's spirited rendition. It shot up the charts, hitting number one. The album that followed was called *The Twelve-Year-Old Genius.* Stevie was 13 by now, but Gordy felt he'd sell more records if the public thought Stevie was still only 12. Stevie was rocking, and suddenly everyone had heard of him. Stevie was a star.

Right around this time, Stevie's trademark soprano voice began to break. Motown could mask it in concert by pairing him with other singers, but it couldn't be hidden in recordings. The good news was that Stevie's new, deeper voice was a rich tenor, and it opened up an exciting range of possibilities in his songs.

Television and movie appearances followed, and soon the Motown traveling show went across the Atlantic to Britain, where the performers had a growing number of fans. By the time Stevie was 15, he'd had another hit ("Uptight") and dropped the "Little" from his nickname. He was too tall to be Little Stevie anymore, and he was starting to take a hand in directing his career. "Uptight" was a sign of things to come—a joyful, catchy tune that was pure Stevie. A reviewer for *Rolling Stone* magazine once wrote that Stevie's music "makes your ears happy, again and again." It was an expression of the love of life bubbling up inside him, so contagious that it was hard to listen to without dancing.

Stevie graduated from high school in 1969 with his musical abilities honed to a fine edge. When he turned 21, Motown handed over the money they'd been keeping in trust for him and Stevie moved to New York.

WHAT HAPPENED NEXT

In the 1970s, Stevie Wonder's music took off in a new direction. He was a pioneer in using the Moog synthesizer, an invention that could reproduce the sounds of many instruments. Today, audiences still rave about his streetwise lyrics and dynamic performances. With

Stevie's joyous spirit continues to delight audiences around the world.

more than 35 albums and 30 top-10 hits, he has won many awards over the years, including 22 Grammys. A sophisticated songwriter, a skillful instrumentalist (he plays the harmonica, piano, synthesizer, drums, organ, and bass guitar), and an innovator in composing and recording music, Stevie Wonder has become one of the most influential musicians of our time.

Over the years, Stevie has used his wealth and fame to help other people. He has been involved in the fight against AIDS, the campaign to end apartheid in South Africa, and relief for victims of Hurricane Katrina in New Orleans. He also started a school for blind and disabled children.

Stevie has been married twice and has seven children. His present wife is Kai Milla Morris, a fashion designer, and his youngest child, Mandla, was born in 2005. When his first daughter, Aisha, was born in 1976, Stevie wrote a song for her that became a hit, "Isn't She Lovely?" Now that Aisha is grown up and a musician herself, she sometimes sings with her father on recordings and in public performances.

Stevie Wonder has maintained his curiosity, which drives him to explore new ways to make music. He is still making both ears and hearts happy all over the world.

SPEND MORE TIME WITH STEVIE

Recorded Live: The Twelve-Year-Old Genius, 1963
This CD includes the live recording of "Fingertips." This song is so much fun to listen to: find it!

Uptight (Everything's Alright), 1966
On this album Stevie is starting to develop his individual sound, as can be heard in the title song. You can also find his version of the peace anthem "Blowin' in the Wind" here.

At the Close of the Century, 1999
This is a set of four CDs featuring Stevie's best songs from the first four decades of his career, including his Motown hits.

Wikipedia is a great source to find out more about Stevie Wonder's music and career. A complete list of all his songs and albums can be found here: http://en.wikipedia.org/wiki/Stevie_Wonder_discography #Albums. You can follow the links to individual songs and discover some fascinating trivia about how the songs were written and details about other artists who have recorded them.

THE DANCING PAINTBRUSH

Wang Yani

1975–

Many children have imaginary friends. Wang Yani had thousands, but they weren't invisible. Her playmates were monkeys who sang, laughed, stole fruit, played tricks on each other, and performed acrobatics. Day after day, Yani painted them on rice paper, using india ink and traditional Chinese paintbrushes. Her lively creations were so impressive that by the time she was 14 she had presented exhibitions of her work in China, Japan, Europe, and North America.

Yani was born in 1975 in Gongcheng, a small town in southern China. Her mother worked in a toy store and her father was an artist. When she was two and a half, her father, Wang Shiqiang, took her into his studio to play while he painted. She picked up a piece of charcoal and started scribbling all over the wall. Instead of getting mad, her father gave her a pencil and some paper. That didn't keep her happy for very long, though; she wanted to help him paint his pictures. He gave her a brush with no paint on it, so that she wouldn't mess up his work. But one day while her father was out of the room, Yani got into the paints and decorated a painting he had been working on for a week. When he came back and saw his project ruined, Shiqiang lost his temper. He yelled at his daughter, who kept crying, "I want to paint and paint."

Finally, Yani's father gave in, allowing her some paint and paper. At first what she produced was much the same as any other two-year-old's efforts—a jumble of lines on the page. But these lines soon began to take on recognizable forms: a bridge, a mountain, a cat. Every picture had a story behind it.

When Yani was three, her father took her to a zoo. There she saw monkeys for the first time. She jumped up and down with excitement, then insisted on staying for hours, watching the monkeys and playing with them by making faces, shrieking, and running. She cried when she had to go home.

When Yani was five, she painted this picture and
called it *Little Monkeys and Mummy*.

"When you pick up a brush don't even ask anyone for help. Because the most wonderful thing about painting is being left alone with your own imagination. I do not paint to get praise from others, but to play a game of endless joy."

Yani began to paint monkeys. At first they looked like the cats she drew, but soon they became distinctly themselves, with dancing legs and arms and curling tails. They appeared in all sorts of situations: riding on the backs of cranes, teasing a lion, climbing trees. Her father bought her a pet monkey, Lida, and Yani adored her. However, she eventually came to prefer her painted monkeys because she could make them do anything she wanted.

Traditionally in China, children are taught that the group is more important than the individual. But Yani's father opposed this idea, giving Yani the freedom to paint whatever she liked. He encouraged his daughter to express what was inside her and to paint the world as she experienced it. Once Yani drew a tree with her two favorite kinds of fruit growing on it. It didn't matter that the tree wasn't realistic—it made sense to her.

Yani used her art almost like a diary. When she was sad, her monkeys cried; when she was happy, they danced and played. If she was hungry, she painted a monkey eating a piece of fruit. Once, worried about getting a needle from the doctor, Yani painted a scared little monkey. Sometimes she painted other animals too: roosters playing tag, peacocks dancing, fish, and camels.

When Yani was four, her paintings were shown in three big cities in China: Beijing, Shanghai, and Guangzhou. Her fame spread quickly throughout the world. Yani used the traditional Chinese

Welcome to the Year of the Rabbit.
By the time she was 11, Yani enjoyed painting
many other animals besides monkeys.

method of painting, but people were captivated by her fresh, expressive style and the sophistication of her technique. International exhibits followed, and Yani and her father spent a lot of time traveling.

Yani would have preferred to stay home, quietly working at her painting. But there were some advantages to her trips: she went to Disneyland in Japan and visited museums in London. She kept painting no matter where she was, even on trains. Meeting new people and talking to reporters was not easy for Yani, who preferred to communicate through her art. When she had a brush in her hand, she forgot about everything else: friends, family—even food. But it was good for her confidence to meet strangers, and she gradually grew more self-assured. Back at home, her father helped her to become more outgoing by getting her involved in sports and other outdoor activities.

When Yani was ready to start a painting, she would sit quietly for a few minutes, focusing her mind. Then she would dribble some paint onto the paper and do a couple of brushstrokes. She never knew what the painting would be about before she started; Yani followed the brush wherever it led her, to create a story. She liked to work listening to classical music, dancing around the room sometimes and singing.

In her teens, Yani kept on giving exhibitions all over the world. She particularly liked her trips to Germany. After spending three years in Beijing learning German, she got a scholarship to study art in Munich. There she met and married another artist, Wu Min, and they had a baby girl.

Yani continues to make vibrant art. She has left her monkeys and animals behind to work with more abstract themes and experiment with color. Her paintbrush continues to dance, but it tells a different story now that she is grown up.

SPEND MORE TIME WITH YANI

A Young Painter: The life and paintings of Wang Yani—China's extraordinary young artist by Zheng Zhensun and Alice Low
This account of Yani's life is illustrated by a lively selection of paintings she did between the ages of two and fifteen, and by photographs of Yani and her family.

THE MOZART OF MATH

Terence Tao

1975–

erry laughed and clapped his hands.

Count Von Count finished counting and threw back his head, laughing like a maniac: "HA-HA-HA-HA-HA!!!" Thunder crashed and lightning flashed across the TV screen.

"1, 2, 3, 4, 5, 6, 7, 8, 9, 10," repeated Terry. "HA-HA-HA-HA-HA!!!" The Count was so funny.

Cookie Monster appeared with a big cookie in his hand. The cookie had the letter B in the middle. Cookie Monster tried not to eat it, but he couldn't help himself. The crumbs scattered as he stuffed it into his mouth.

"B," said Terry. Now the B was bouncing around the screen, with the letters A L L.

"BALL," sang Terry. "The letter B. Ball."

Sesame Street ended, and Terry's mother came into the room.

"Show's over," she said, putting out her hand to him. "Come and play with me in the kitchen while I make lunch."

Terry got up and clutched his mother's hand. "Cookie," he said. "I want a cookie."

Grace laughed. "You're my own little cookie monster, aren't you?"

As she stirred the soup, Terry began to play with the magnets on the fridge. He found a blue 2 and a green 3 and put them side by side. Then he went looking for the rest of the numbers. They were all mixed in with alphabet letters.

Soon he had all the numbers lined up. "1, 2, 3, 4, 5, 6, 7, 8, 9, 10!" he shouted. "HA-HA-HA-HA-HA!"

His mother turned down the soup and came over to kneel beside him.

"Good work, Terry," she said. "Now try this." She took away the 1 and the 3.

Terry chuckled. This was his favorite game. He reached up and took away the 5, the 7, and the 9.

"2, 4, 6, 8, 10," he said, and looked at his mother. She nodded and gave him back the 1 and the 3. He lined them up with the other odd numbers. "1, 3, 5, 7, 9," he muttered. Then he removed the 2 from the other line of numbers and put it between the 1 and the 3. He looked at his mother.

"Yes," she said, smiling. "1 plus 2 makes ..."

"3!" he said. He moved the 2 to go between the 3 and the 5. "3 plus 2 makes ..." He looked at his mother.

"5," she answered.

Terry laughed. They sat together playing with the magnetic numbers for a while. Then Grace remembered the soup and jumped up to check it.

Terry stayed in front of the fridge, staring at the numbers.

"What do you see, Terry?" asked Grace. Her son had a faraway look in his eyes. He rearranged the numbers again. Then he reached out and touched the 2.

"Two," he said. "I'm two."

"That's right, you are," said Grace. "Come and have lunch."

OPEN CHANNEL

Wolfgang Amadeus Mozart, the legendary child prodigy, seemed to have an open channel to the world of music. Glorious music flowed out of him. In the 20th century a little boy in Australia had a similar connection to the mysterious world of numbers: equations and formulas tumbled out of his head. Today Terry Tao is in his 30s. His genius for math is as great as Mozart's for music, and his accomplishments are just as amazing.

MAGNETIC NUMBERS

Terry Tao and his parents, Billy and Grace Tao, lived in a suburb of Adelaide, a large city on the southern coast of Australia. Like many children around the world in the 1970s, Terry loved to watch *Sesame Street*. He would sit on the living room carpet playing with his toys and laughing at the puppets. Even though Terry was not yet two years old, he paid close attention to everything that was happening on the screen.

One day, while Terry was playing with a friend's alphabet blocks, his parents noticed that he was carefully putting them in alphabetical order, then spelling out words. Terry had learned to read from watching *Sesame Street*. He had also learned how to count, and soon he was doing simple arithmetic, adding and subtracting. He had lots of toys, but he wasn't very interested in cars or trains. Terry's favorite playthings were the magnetic numbers on the fridge. He thought math was a wonderful game, and he loved the patterns the numbers made as he arranged and rearranged them in different sequences.

Grace and Billy Tao encouraged Terry by providing him with books, including some about math. Terry gobbled them up and asked for more. His parents could hardly keep up with his burning desire for knowledge. Once they found him sitting at a typewriter in his father's office. He had just finished copying out a whole page from a children's book, typing with one finger.

The Taos realized their son had an extraordinary mind. They wanted to help him develop his abilities, but they were also cautious. They didn't want him to lose out on his childhood.

NURTURING A GENIUS

If Terry Tao could have chosen the perfect parents to raise him as a happy, healthy, well-adjusted child prodigy, chances are he would have chosen Billy and Grace Tao.

The Taos immigrated to Australia from Hong Kong in 1972, three years before Terry was born. Terry's father was a pediatrician, a doctor who works with children. Terry's mother won first-class honors at university studying math and physics, then taught math in high schools. Terry was their first child, and he was soon followed by two brothers, Trevor and Nigel.

Some parents with a gifted child try to take the credit for their child's talents. Other parents put the interests of the child first; they create a loving environment in which the child can learn and grow. Terry's parents had no desire to gain fame through their son. But once they realized Terry's astonishing abilities, Billy and Grace threw themselves enthusiastically into the job of giving Terry what he needed. Grace quickly realized it was best to guide Terry rather than to teach him. He didn't like to be told what to do in math, but preferred to follow his nose. His mother provided him with math textbooks and lots of stimulation, and then she let Terry learn at his own pace. It turned out that his own pace was very, very fast.

WHIZ KID

With his parents' steady encouragement, Terry advanced by leaps and bounds. By the time he was three, he was reading and doing math at a six-year-old's level.

Fascinated with the world of math, Terry spent hours and hours learning more about numbers. He was endlessly curious, and liked nothing better than sitting down and attacking a math problem. When he was four, his parents asked Miraca Gross, an education specialist, to test Terry on his math skills. To Ms. Gross's surprise, Terry could multiply two-digit numbers (such as 48 x 64) in his head. She had to work out the solutions on paper to see if Terry's answers were right. Needless to say, they were.

Test Your Smarts

Here's a math problem Terry aced one month before he turned five. See how you do with it.

Look at the series of numbers below. There is a hidden pattern. If the series were to continue, what would the next four numbers be?
    9182736
(See page 129 for the answer.)

SPEEDING THROUGH SCHOOL

Terry was three and a half when he started grade one at a private school. All the other children were five. Terry was ahead of the other kids in his class in math and reading, but he still acted like a three-year-old. He distracted the other pupils and didn't really fit in. After a few weeks Terry's parents and the teachers at the school decided it would be best if Terry left.

His parents found a local school with a kindergarten for kids the same age as Terry. The principal was open to their ideas about Terry's education, and the new school was a much better fit for the bright little boy. Terry did all the regular kindergarten activities, but at home he studied math with Grace. His progress was phenomenal: by Terry's fifth birthday he had mastered most of the grade school math it took ordinary kids seven years to complete.

With the help of the school's friendly principal, Grace and Billy found a way to tailor Terry's schooling. They decided Terry would take classes at different levels for different subjects. That way he could advance quickly in the subjects he was really good at, but still spend time every day with kids his own age.

Terry, age eight, kneels at the big desk to write a math test with grade 11 students.

The Taos lived within driving distance of a primary school, a high school, and a university. Grace ferried Terry between schools so he could juggle his classes. By the time Terry was eight, he was studying math with grade 12 students, learning physics with grade 11s, doing English and social studies with grade 8s, and taking all his other subjects at primary school. This system worked well, creating a balance between Terry's brains and his social skills.

At first the little boy saw nothing strange about his schedule. Since his classes had always been at different levels, it seemed natural to him. He made friends with kids his own age and got on well with the older students. His parents tried to get him interested in sports and music, but Terry was never very enthusiastic about those activities. He kept coming back to computer games, science, and his beloved math.

After school, Terry would often read math textbooks for three or four hours. One book led him to another, and he followed his instincts about what to study next. At age five he started delving into computer manuals. Soon he had taught himself BASIC, a computer language used to write programs. By the time he turned six, he had written several computer programs of his own. One was about Fibonacci numbers, a sequence of special numbers named after Leonardo Fibonacci, an Italian mathematician. Terry's instructions reveal his playful side. He talks about Mr. Fibonacci being in heaven at one point, and he signs off by having Mr. Fibonacci drive away: "Here goes his car: brmmmm-brmmmm-putt-putt-vraow-chatter-chatter!"

MAKING FRIENDS AND LOSING LUNCHES

Although Terry could handle advanced schoolwork, he had trouble keeping track of his belongings as he moved from class to class. He lost lunch boxes, pens, pencils, books, calculators, and at least one brand new sweater. Later his principal gave him a copy of a note he had written in his diary about Terry's absentmindedness. Terry kept this note for years because it made him laugh.

> *Terry used to come to me for maths after he had been to another teacher for Reading and another for Spelling. He often lost something in each place or on the way from room to room. One day he arrived for maths completely empty-handed. He had lost the lot. He came into the classroom and announced almost tearfully, "I don't know where anything is."*

Despite his forgetfulness, Terry adapted well to his topsy-turvy schedule. After the initial weirdness of having him in their class, the older kids accepted Terry and didn't give him a hard time about being a whiz kid. If anything, they felt protective towards him. Terry's parents discouraged him from becoming conceited, and he never acted as if he was better than other kids.

INDOOR TOBOGGANING

Terry wasn't the only child in the Tao family with special educational needs. About the time Terry learned to read and count, his little brother Trevor was born. When Trevor was two, the Taos discovered he was autistic. This is a medical condition that affects learning and behavior. Trevor was slow in learning how to talk, and he needed patient coaching from his parents and from a specialist who came to work with him five days a week.

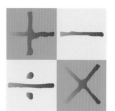

Nigel, Terry's youngest brother, was born two years after Trevor. As they grew up, the three boys became very close. They spent most of their time playing with each other, and sometimes even finished each other's sentences. Sometimes they got up to mischief. Once they took their father's mattress off his bed and used it as a toboggan to go down the stairs. They kicked a football around, watched Jackie Chan movies, and played endless computer games together. When they got older, they all learned to play bridge, a complicated card game. There was lots of friendly competition among the three boys, even to the point of seeing who was best at cracking the eggs when their father showed them how to cook breakfast.

Terry (middle) and his brothers Nigel (left) and Trevor (right).

Terry taught Trevor to play chess, and Trevor caught on so quickly that he was soon beating his brother every time they played. Trevor developed into a chess prodigy, later representing Australia at international competitions. He also turned out to be a talented musician. Both Trevor and Nigel excelled at math, and each of them was good enough to compete in the International Mathematical Olympiad.

Terry's dad was hard at work all day as a doctor, so it fell to his mom to run the house, keep pace with Terry's challenging schedule and with Trevor's needs, and still find time for little Nigel.

LETTING OFF STEAM

Somehow the Taos managed to give each of their three children lots of care and attention. But it wasn't easy for anyone. Every so often the stress got to Terry. If he couldn't figure out the answer to a math question, he would throw his pen on the floor, tear up the paper, and go to his bedroom to sulk. He refused to talk to anyone and would yell at his brothers.

When Terry's father was there, he would tell a joke to cheer Terry up. If his mom had a moment, she would sit down to help him. But often Terry would calm down and go back to the problem himself. The second time around, it usually didn't seem so difficult.

To let off steam, Terry liked to jump on the family trampoline that was built into the deck in the backyard. Playing with his brothers relaxed him, too. However, he developed the habit of chewing the tops of ballpoint pens as he worked, reducing them to mangled bits of plastic. Finally his mother bought him a rubber doggie bone to chew on instead. It tasted so awful that his pen-chewing habit was cured.

When he started high school classes, at age seven, one of Terry's teachers encouraged him to write in a journal about his feelings and ideas. She would read what he had written, then write back to him. Terry wrote about how difficult it was rushing from one class to another and being expected to know so many different things, and about how his brothers sometimes bugged him and scribbled on his work. His teacher agreed that life could be hard, but she told him he could turn his frustrations and failures into something positive by looking at what they taught him. Terry took her words to heart.

Get Messy!

Miss Frizzell, a science teacher on the television show *The Magic School Bus*, always encouraged her students to learn by taking chances, making mistakes, and getting messy. Encouraged by his own teachers, Terry Tao followed the same principle. Even today, he talks about the joy of persisting with a math problem until he finally figures it out. Arriving at the answer is extremely satisfying, but making mistakes is part of the journey. Sometimes Terry will get an idea for a solution and then, after working on it for weeks, realize that he was going in the wrong direction. When that happens, he goes back to the beginning and starts again.

ALWAYS CHECK YOUR WORK

Terry began to enter math contests at a young age. It wasn't always smooth sailing for him, though. He had to learn some basic lessons the hard way, such as "Always check your work," "Don't be over-confident," and, when writing exams, "Watch the clock." Once, when Terry was about eight, he wrote an exam for a math competition and finished early—in just 20 minutes for what was supposed to be a two-hour exam. Instead of reviewing his answers for mistakes, Terry spent the rest of the time doing something much more interesting: figuring out a method for calculating the value of pi (π). When his mother suggested after the exam that he should have checked his answers, Terry said, "Just wait till I win the prize." But Terry didn't win the prize, and he felt pretty depressed about it. Later, his father looked over his test and found that most of Terry's mistakes were in arithmetic (adding, subtracting, multiplication, or division) and could have easily been corrected. After that, Terry always tried to check his work.

HE SHOOTS! HE SCORES!

Terry broke quite a few records with his high scores on tests. His IQ (Intelligence Quotient: a way of measuring intelligence) was measured at 220—a startling figure, considering that the average IQ is 100. Only one person in a million has an IQ as high as Terry's.

When Terry was eight years old, he took the Australian university entrance math exams. He scored 90 percent on one test and 85 percent on the other. Seven months later he took the SAT math exam. This is a university entrance test that kids in the United States take when they are 17 or 18. Terry scored 760 out of 800. Only 1 percent of all students taking the test score higher than 750.

TWO PIECES OF CHOCOLATE

Terry's father tells a good story about how Terry celebrated his incredibly high SAT scores when he was eight. Billy asked his son what he'd like as a reward for doing so well. Terry gave it some thought. He seemed to be having a hard time coming up with something he really wanted. At last he smiled and said, "Dad, you know that chocolate we've been saving in the fridge? Let's eat it." So he fetched the chocolate from the kitchen, broke it into two pieces, and gave one to his dad while he ate the other. Then he went back to the math problem he had been working on.

The Taos encouraged Terry to enjoy his success, but they never made a big fuss about winning. They realized that each of his accomplishments was a stepping stone to his future, and there would always be a fresh challenge ahead. They kept in mind an old Chinese saying: "Beyond the tall mountain in front of you there is always another, taller mountain."

HIGH-STAKES COMPETITION

Terry tried out for the International Mathematical Olympiad when he was nine. Although all the other contestants were senior high school students, his score was the highest in South Australia, and Terry ranked sixth in the whole country. When he moved to the national level, however, he didn't make the cut.

It wasn't easy to lose his chance to compete. But his father felt that Terry's failure in the contest was sending an important message. Billy compared Terry's rapid advancement to grass that grows so fast that it doesn't have time to develop strong roots. He felt his son needed to develop a deeper knowledge of math. Terry went back to his books.

At age 10, Terry tried out for the Math Olympiad again. This time he did brilliantly, placing on the Australian team that traveled to Warsaw, Poland, for the final round. He won a bronze medal there, and a silver medal the following year in Havana, Cuba. In 1988, when he was just 13, Terry became the youngest contestant ever to win a gold medal. That year the Olympiad was held in Australia, which made his victory all the sweeter.

Terry had his picture taken with the Australian prime minister, and a few articles about him appeared in Australian newspapers. But his parents didn't want him to become too well known because they thought it would make life harder for him. They succeeded in keeping Terry out of the spotlight for most of his childhood.

In His Own Words

"I may be labeled as an intelligent child by some of my teachers, but I still have a long way to go yet before I can become as wise as any one of you here today."
—from "My Recollections," a speech Terry gave to educators and students at Purdue University in 1985, when he was 10

How Hard is the Math Olympiad?

Contestants in the International Math Olympiad must be still in high school and under the age of 20. The six brightest math students from each country are chosen by competition, and then they go up against the wiliest math whizzes from about 90 other countries.

The contest takes place over two days. Each day the contestants get three problems and are allowed four and a half hours to solve them. The problems are based on high school math, including geometry, number theory, algebra, and combinatorics. The solutions demand fiendish ingenuity backed by solid mathematical skills.

Held in a different location each year, the Math Olympiad is fun but nerve-racking for the chosen few who qualify. The competitors meet kids from all over the world with similar interests, and they get to travel to a new and interesting place. Oh yes, and they also have the opportunity to test their wits on some gritty math problems.

THE TURNING POINT

When Terry was nine, he started taking first-year physics and second-year math classes at Flinders University. He was still in a range of high school classes, from grade 9 English to grade 12 chemistry. Terry was also whizzing along in Latin, which he had taken up because he had some spare time.

Now that Terry was ready for university courses, he and his family had a serious decision to make about his future. He could easily have aimed to graduate from university at a ridiculously young age—perhaps 11—then gone on to do graduate work at one of the world's top universities. But Billy and Grace were cautious. Terry was a little boy. A smart little boy, to be sure, but still a child. He needed his brothers and his parents in his life, as well as friends his own age to fool around with.

Terry's parents took him on a three-week trip to the United States when he was 10, to tour several universities and talk to educators about what path might be best for him. Terry prepared a speech about his life to deliver to a select audience at Purdue University. He called it "My Recollections," and today it provides a charming glimpse into Terry's personality at that age. He was a funny, unassuming kid who could laugh at himself and tell a good story. He talked about how frightening it was when he got separated from his mother in the London subway when he was seven, and how he sometimes put on one sock but forgot about the other.

After consulting leading experts in the fields of both math and gifted children, the Taos returned to Adelaide and reached their verdict: Terry would carry on with his current schedule rather than enroll full-time at a university. Grace and Billy didn't want to rush him. It was clear that the system of staggering his classes was working; for all his brilliance, Terry was still remarkably normal and well adjusted.

Terry graduated from Flinders University at the age of 17, with both a bachelor's and a master's degree. With a Fulbright Scholarship under his arm, he set off for Princeton University in New Jersey, to work on his Ph.D. It was a long way from home, but by then Terry was ready. His family had given him all the loving support and encouragement he needed to grow up to be a happy genius.

Terry grew up in Adelaide, a beautiful city on the southern coast of Australia.

Math and Music

Terry Tao's special field of expertise is harmonic analysis. This is one of the places where Mozart's music meets Terry's math. In music, harmonics are the different tones you hear in one note. Sound travels in waves, and these waves can be measured using math. The study of various kinds of waves is called harmonics. Waves are a method of transmitting energy, and they are found in radio signals, electricity, microwaves, and light.

Terry Tao sees many similarities between music and math. For example, it all comes down to practicing. Just as a musician must practice scales and finger exercises for many years to master her technique, a mathematician must practice math for years before he can make great discoveries. Practicing the skills of math can be boring sometimes. To help high school students appreciate just how fascinating the subject can be, Terry wrote a math textbook when he was 15. It explains how to do problems like the ones he faced in the Math Olympiads.

WHAT HAPPENED NEXT

Many of Terry Tao's great achievements still lie before him. However, his accomplishments to date are so dazzling that he has already made his mark.

Terry earned his Ph.D. by the time he was 20. He moved to the University of California, Los Angeles (UCLA), where he became a full professor at the unlikely age of 24. There he remains, teaching students and working on the cutting edge of 21st-century math. He has a worldwide reputation among advanced students as the guy to call when you have a real dilly of a math problem. He married an American, Laura Kim Tao, and they have a little boy, William.

Terry has received a string of awards and prizes for his ground-breaking work. In 2006 he won the Fields Medal, which is given only once every four years. Known as the Nobel Prize of the math world, it was awarded to him in Madrid, Spain, where he was

mobbed by the press and his fans as if he were a rock star. In typical Terry fashion, he was a bit awed by all the attention and eager to get back to the real fun: his latest work in the field of harmonic analysis.

Terry remains modest about his talent. Many of his discoveries are so advanced that they won't be used in any practical sense until the rest of the world catches up to him—in 20, 30, or even 100 years. But Terry sees math as a group effort: great mathematicians throughout history help each other by building up the layers of knowledge. He hopes that the breakthroughs he is making will lay the groundwork for more math discoveries in the future. Meanwhile, numbers, theorems, progressions, and algorithms continue to dance around in his brain.

It's Not Magic

Harmonic analysis. Needles. Honeycombs. Algorithms. Progressions. Cosmic distance ladder. Prime numbers.

As a mathematician, Terry Tao works with these things every day. They may seem like mysterious concepts to most of us, but Terry understands that math makes the world go round. "It's not magic," he explains. "Using math ... you can see where all of science comes from, and a lot of technology ... You realize that the world is not this incomprehensible scary place, it's actually just built out of very simple, logical ideas."

Here are some examples:

- Prime numbers keep money safe in ATM machines.
- The cosmic distance ladder uses high school math to calculate the distance between stars.
- The creators of Google invented special algorithms to design their Internet search engine.

Breaking the Code at Day Care

One day while he was waiting to pick up his son, William, at day care, Terry ran into another father, Emmanuel Candes, who is also a brainy mathematician. They got to talking about their favorite subject, and soon they were discussing ways to decode broken signals. If a message was coming through in bits and pieces, were there mathematical formulas that could help to reconstruct the whole message? Their conversation was interrupted by their children, who needed to be taken home, but later the two dads got together and continued their speculation. Working with geometry, statistics, and a form of math called calculus, they constructed a theory that proved to be a winner. Now, CIA agents tapping phones and doctors trying to figure out brain scans can get the whole story by using the theory that began as small talk between two dads at day care.

Answer to "Test Your Smarts"

All of the numbers are multiples of 9: 9, 18, 27, and 36.
The next four numbers would be 4554.

SPEND MORE TIME WITH TERRY

http://www.ucla.edu/player/terence-tao/index.html
Go to Terry's website and watch a video of him talking about how much fun it is to find the answers. While Terry talks, you can see pictures of him as a little boy. Appropriately enough, the music of Mozart plays in the background.

Solving Mathematical Problems: A Personal Perspective by Terence Tao
If you're keen on math, get a copy of this textbook Terry wrote when he was 15.

SOURCES

Phillis Wheatley

Gates, Henry Louis. 2002 Jefferson Lecture in the Humanities.
    http://www.neh.gov/whoweare/gates/lecture.html.
Lasky, Kathryn. *A Voice of Her Own: The Story of Phillis Wheatley, Slave Poet.*
    Cambridge, MA: Candlewick Press, 2003.
Richmond, Merle. *Phillis Wheatley, Poet.* American Women of Achievement Series.
    New York: Chelsea House Publishers, 1988.
Robinson, William H. *Phillis Wheatley and Her Writings.* New York: Garland
    Publishing, 1984.
Weidt, Maryann N. *Revolutionary Poet: A Story About Phillis Wheatley.* Minneapolis:
    Carolrhoda Books, 1997.
Wheatley, Phillis. *Complete Writings.* Edited by Vincent Carretta. New York:
    Penguin Books, 2001.
http://www.bbc.co.uk/worldservice/africa/features/storyofafrica/index_section9.shtml

Maria Agnesi

http://www-history.mcs.st-andrews.ac.uk/history/Biographies/Agnesi.html
http://mathworld.wolfram.com/WitchofAgnesi.html
http://en.wikipedia.org/wiki/Maria_Agnesi
http://womenshistory.about.com/library/bio/blbio_maria_agnesi.htm

Clara Schumann

Macy, Sheryl. *Two Romantic Trios: The story of six passionate people who changed
    the world of music.* Portland, OR: Allegro Publishing, 1991.
Reich, Nancy B. *Clara Schumann: The Artist and the Woman.* Ithaca, NY:
    Cornell University Press, 1985.
Reich, Susanna. *Clara Schumann, Piano Virtuoso.* New York: Clarion Books, 1999.

Fanny Mendelssohn

Kamen, Gloria. *Hidden Music: The Life of Fanny Mendelssohn.* New York:
    Simon and Schuster, 1996.
Kupferberg, Herbert. *The Mendelssohns: Three Generations of Genius.* New York:
    Scribners, 1972.

Buster Keaton

Blesh, Rudi. *Keaton.* New York: MacMillan, 1966.
Dardis, Tom. *Keaton: The Man Who Wouldn't Lie Down.* New York: Scribners, 1979.
Keaton, Buster, and Charles Samuels. *My Wonderful World of Slapstick.* New York:
    Da Capo, Doubleday, 1960.
Knopf, Robert. *The Theater and Cinema of Buster Keaton.* Princeton, NJ: Princeton
    University Press, 1999.
Meade, Marion. *Buster Keaton: Cut to the Chase.* New York: HarperCollins, 1995.

Dai Vernon

Ben, David. *Dai Vernon: A Biography.* Toronto: Magicana, 2006.

Dai Vernon: The Spirit of Magic. The Canadians: Biographies of a Nation series. Video produced by Great North Productions in association with History Television and the CRB Foundation's Heritage Project, 1999.

Erdnase, S.W. *The Expert at the Card Table: A Treatise on the Science and Art of Manipulating Cards.* First printed 1902.

Johnson, Karl. *The Magician and the Cardsharp.* New York: Henry Holt, 2005.

http://en.wikipedia.org/wiki/Dai_Vernon

Stevie Wonder

Davis, Sharon. *Stevie Wonder: Rhythms of Wonder.* London: Robson Books, 2003.

Green, William Sanford Carl. *Stevie Wonder.* Mankato, MN: Crestwood House, 1986.

Swenson, John. *Stevie Wonder.* London: Plexus, 1986.

Wilson, Beth P. *Stevie Wonder.* New York: Putnam, 1979.

http://www.steviewonder.net/

Wang Yani

Zheng Zhensun and Alice Low. *A Young Painter: The life and paintings of Wang Yani—China's extraordinary young artist.* New York: Scholastic, 1991.

Terry Tao

Bevan, Scott (reporter). "Terry Tao compared with science greats." Transcript from television program *The 7:30 Report*, broadcast September 27, 2006. Australian Broadcasting Corporation. http://www.abc.net.au/7.30/content/2006/s1750564.htm.

Colvin, Mark (reporter). "Maths needs marketing, says Fields Medallist." Transcript from radio program *PM*, broadcast September 28, 2006, by the Australian Broadcasting Corporation.

Gross, Miraca. "Radical acceleration in Australia: Terence Tao." Davidson Institute's GT Cybersource. G/C/T, Prufrock Press. July/August 1986. http://www.gt-cybersource.org/Record.aspx?NavID=2_0&rid=11273.

Smith, Deborah. "What can parents do with a child genius?" *Sydney Herald*, August 26, 2006. http://www.smh.com.au/news/national/mozart-of-maths/2006/08/25/1156012745894.html?page=fullpage#contentSwap2.

Tao, Billy. "Through the Looking-Glass: From a Parent's Perspective of Giftedness That Leads to a Three-Dimensional Model." Unpublished article. April 2005.

Tao, Terry. "My Recollections." Talk given in 1985 to a group of university students and educators. The event was sponsored by Prof. Grayson Wheatley, Professor of Mathematical Education at Purdue University.

Tao, Terry. Website at University of California, Los Angeles. http://www.math.ucla.edu/~tao/.

NOTES

page 11   "Did Fear and Danger ..." Phillis Wheatley, "On Messrs Hussey and
           Coffin," http://oldpoetry.com/opoem/show/43998-Phillis-Wheatley-
           On-Messrs-Hussey-and-Coffin.

page 22   "In every Breast ..." Phillis Wheatley, *Complete Writings*, ed. Vincent
           Carretta (New York: Penguin Books, 2001), 153.

page 31   "For if at any time ..."
           http://instructional1.calstatela.edu/sgray/Agnesi/Quotes/Quotes.html

page 43   "She plays with as much strength ..." Susanna Reich, *Clara Schumann,
           Piano Virtuoso* (New York: Clarion Books, 1999), 95.

page 52   "When I am able to practice ..." Reich, *Clara Schumann*, 97.

page 53   "Although we had many disagreements ..." Reich, *Clara Schumann*, 77.

page 57   "It must be a sign of talent ..."
           http://quote.robertgenn.com/auth_search.php?name=fanny+
           mendelssohn

page 76   "Because I was also a born hambone ..." Buster Keaton and Charles
           Samuels, *My Wonderful World of Slapstick* (New York: Da Capo,
           Doubleday, 1960), 13.

page 84   "I was born to deceive." Karl Johnson, *The Magician and the
           Cardsharp* (New York: Henry Holt, 2005), 11.

page 101   "Many years ago ..." Lynn Norment, "Stevie Wonder Returns!" *Ebony*,
           July 2004.

page 102   "makes your ears happy ..." Jon Pareles, *Rolling Stone* 459 (1985).

page 108   "When you pick up a brush ..."
           http://www.myhero.com/myhero/hero.asp?hero=w_yani

page 119   "Terry used to come to me ..." Terry Tao, "My Recollections," talk
           given in 1985 to a group of university students and educators at
           Purdue University, West Lafayette, Indiana.

page 128   "Using math ..." Mark Colvin, reporter, "Maths needs marketing, says
           Fields Medallist," transcript from radio program *PM*, broadcast
           September 28, 2006, by the Australian Broadcasting Corporation.
           Used with permission.

INDEX